MANDALAY

For Thida and Zeyar

Much as I love you tiny humans all
the way to the moon and back, I'm
looking forward to when it's finally
your turn to cook for me, and
hopefully this book will help.

xxx

MiMi Aye

MANDALAY

Recipes and Tales
from a Burmese Kitchen

Photography by
Cristian Barnett

BLOOMSBURY PUBLISHING
LONDON · OXFORD · NEW YORK · NEW DELHI · SYDNEY

Contents

Introduction

First things first. Burma or Myanmar? Myanmar or Burma?

Apart from the fact that it's always made me wince a little to hear people butcher the pronunciation of the official name (for the avoidance of doubt, it's '*M'yun-mar*', not '*MY-an-mar*'), I have always called my motherland Burma, simply because that's how I've always known it – even in the Burmese language, it was referred to as *Bamar-pyi*.

I should qualify that to say my *spiritual* motherland, since, whereas my father and both brothers were all born in Mandalay in Upper Burma, and my mother in Mogok near the Shan State, I myself was born in the slightly more prosaic seaside town of Margate in England. But, ever since I was a little girl, as my parents are Burmese through and through, and most of my family still live there, they have taken us back to visit their homeland year after year. In some ways, I feel like I grew up there, so it's natural that I should feel a strong affinity with the place.

Beginnings

My folks, especially my mother, had a deathly fear that I would somehow end up rejecting my 'Burmeseness' so, in order to instil a 'proper' sense of culture, they taught me the beautiful Burmese language with its winsome and bubble-like script, raised us as strict-ish Buddhists and reared us on brilliant Burmese food.

I guess my parents were justifiably anxious that they were fighting a losing battle, as the headmaster of my brothers' school in Kent once summoned them in for a meeting where he forbade us from speaking in Burmese at home, whilst I attended a Catholic convent school run by French nuns called Sister Marie-Antoinette and Sister Denise.

(Beyond) Rangoon

My mother's side is mainly based in the former capital city of Yangon, aka Rangoon (although they're originally from Mogok – of which more later). Whenever we landed at Mingaladon Airport, one of her nieces or nephews would pick us up, and we'd drive straight to my eldest aunt's house near Inya Lake in Yangon, chattering all the way.

When we got there, the table of said family matriarch would be heaving with *Mogok meeshay* noodles and dim sum, gram fritters and Indian sweetmeats, roast duck and sushi, none of them really going together, but all of them favourites or special requests and brought in or made in our honour as guests from abroad.

The air would be thick with raucous laughter as we'd play cards and catch up on juicy gossip and then one of our cousins

would suddenly crack a joke that she'd recently made a million (pyas, that is, which is about £5). Incidentally, there's even an old Burmese rhyme (with its rough translation) that goes:

> *Mandalay ma za-gar;*   *Mandalay for the eloquence;*
> *Yangon ma a-kywar;*   *Yangon for the braggadocio;*
> *Mawlamyine ma a-sar.*   *Mawlamyine for the cuisine.*

Make of that what you will – also note that my father claims that the only remarkable food to come out of Mawlamyine are the massive prawns…

So, my mother's family are lively, brash and lots of fun, which is rather like the town itself. This attitude translates to the food in Yangon – it's modern, slightly flashy, and the first to adopt new trends and to embrace foreign influences. There are hip cafes and bars everywhere, plus a relatively recent influx of chain restaurants, whilst, due to a government crackdown, genuine street food is almost a thing of the past, except in markets or Chinatown.

The first time I saw a Burmese supermarket was in Yangon. Although supermarkets are ten-a-penny back in England, in the Burma of 1998 it seemed truly astonishing. They were so alien that, when a cousin came to stay with us from Burma a few years earlier and we popped to Somerfield for some groceries, she put everything straight in her rucksack because she didn't know that she should use a basket. (At the time I did wonder why a member of staff began following us around.)

I clearly remember when burger joints and spaghetti houses started to open up in Yangon, and thinking how bizarre it was, despite the very Burmese touches such as pickled chillies spiking the silky pasta, or crispy bacon in the burgers comprising more juicy, caramelised fat than lean meat.

The reason for my awe was (and still is) the very peculiar juxtaposition of Westernisation and staunch traditional values. I hesitate to say Buddhist values; whilst 90 per cent of Burma is Theravadin Buddhist, its conservatism is, I believe, a result of 'Burmeseness' (and isolation wrought by the military junta) rather than of Buddhism per se.

For example, both men and women still wear traditional Burmese clothes on a daily basis: patterned sarongs called *longyi*, subdivided as colourful *htamein* for the women and rather more mundane *paso* for the men. Although many men do wear trousers (generally the Shan version known as *Shan baun-bi* aka Thai fisherman pants), until recently women barely wore skirts – at least not ones that revealed more than an ankle – and those that did deign to wear trousers were looked at askance or laughed at or assumed to be from abroad. This is becoming much less the case in Yangon these days, but, for the moment Mandalay keeps things old school.

Even in Yangon though, public displays of affection between couples are often frowned upon, although weirdly, it's fine for

On the way to Mogok near the Shan State by pick-up truck with various family members. Standing in front is one of my mother's brothers – his son is on the right next to my brother and me.

My father cannot resist making me pose with some tribes people that we come across.

those of the same sex to hold hands or link arms – including men – as it's usually assumed that such friendliness must be platonic…

Historically, alcohol has also been considered a bit of a no-no, and this one is specifically discouraged by Theravadin Buddhist precepts – although funnily enough, eating meat is not. And though there has been a recent proliferation of roadside pubs peddling Myanmar beer and rum, and chichi wine bars selling more sophisticated libations, those that frequent them are still often not well thought of. Certainly in the eyes of the older generation, if a Burmese man drinks regularly, he is considered a drunken reprobate, and if a Burmese woman drinks at all, she is deemed beyond the pale.

Smoking, however, is greeted with tolerance, if not approval, for both men and women. Kipling's Burmese maiden and her 'whackin' white cheroot' is still a familiar sight, although nowadays you would have to substitute a grizzled grandmother for the fair 'maiden' (even more so for the old national pastime of betel-chewing), as Yangon's youth is more likely to prefer Lucky Strike.

This strong sense of tradition translates to the Yangon kitchen. Whilst it may be more common to go out for sushi, dim sum or pizza, at home it's usual to have a Burmese menu of rich curries, fragrant rice and saucy noodles, although thanks to the flourishing Indian community in Yangon, a crunchy potato and pea-packed samosa or a crispy onion pakora may appear.

But despite this culinary orthodoxy, Yangon has always been the part of Burma most familiar to someone from the West. If you squinted your eyes, you could almost believe you were in Bangkok or Singapore.

The Road to Mandalay

My father's family hails from Upper Burma, from the much more sedate and old-world town of Mandalay, and this is where most of them still reside, and so, whenever we visited Burma, we'd make the long trek up to see them all, and to stay with my beloved grandparents Daw Tin Tin and U Hla Pe.

The distance from Yangon to Mandalay is similar to that from London to Edinburgh, but modes of transport are decidedly more antiquated in these parts. Yet, although it entailed a fifteen-hour, bone-juddering train trip overnight on the hardest seats known to mankind, to an eight-year-old MiMi with food on her mind, the journey to Mandalay seemed wildly exciting.

At every stop (and there were many), countless smiling and chattering vendors would suddenly spring from nowhere and flock to our open windows, bearing baskets of wondrous things: bunches of sweet, fat, little bananas; strings of prickly rambutan; kettles of steaming green tea; banana-leaf parcels of sticky rice; 'twigs' of chewy goat jerky tied into bundles with straw knots we would have to unpick; and tiny packets of hard-boiled quail eggs, which we would clumsily peel and pop into our mouths one by one, savouring the pale, creamy yolks.

Even now, thirty years later, the journey by train hasn't changed all that much, as chef and writer Anthony Bourdain found out to his cost when he visited Burma for his CNN show *Parts Unknown*.

On our bleary-eyed, early morning arrival, we'd be whisked straight to my grandparents' house in the centre of town for bowl after bowl of *mohinga*, heaped with crispy split-pea fritters, slices of soft duck egg, bouncy fishcakes, roasted chilli flakes and shredded coriander leaves, with salty fish sauce and lemon wedges to squeeze on the side. A bounty of piquant textures and tastes, *mohinga* is a breakfast of fish and rice vermicelli soup, renowned as the national dish of Burma and a firm favourite of my two older brothers.

As someone addicted to rice however, I was more interested in the *see-htamin* that was also given to us – a moreish golden sticky rice scattered with fried onions, gloriously mushy yellow peas and freshly fried fish jerky called *nga-pote chauk* that I'd demolish in seconds when no-one was looking.

The next morning, my grandmother (my *Pwa Pwa*) and her staff would without fail be up at the crack of dawn to cook up huge pots of delicious curry and fluffy rice, in order to give alms to the local monastery. A seemingly endless line of monks would solemnly parade past our house as I attempted to be respectful, ladling out equal portions into their begging bowls whilst simultaneously trying not to drool as the tantalising scent of sweet cinnamon chicken or braised beef curry wafted up to me.

Unsurprisingly, only the choicest ingredients and the leanest meat would be served up to the monks. I remember feeling grief-stricken and emitting an audible wail when my grandfather (*Po Po*) told me they'd thrown out all the fat that they'd removed from the pork belly and bamboo shoot stew, as I'd greedily earmarked the glistening chunks for myself.

Thus, the food at my grandparents' home was always wonderful and plentiful, but where Mandalay really came into its own was *lan-bay zar* – literally 'roadside fare', aka street food. Safety regulations are few and far between in Burma (for example, car seatbelts have yet to properly manifest themselves), but as I mentioned earlier, in Yangon, jobsworths saw fit to sweep away all the roadside vendors and most of the street cafes. However, in Mandalay such places persist and for this I am truly grateful. The rules that have begun to stifle Yangon have failed to fully infiltrate Mandalay – and this holds true in other ways. One example: in Mandalay, cyclists, motorbikes and sidecar rickshaws outnumber the cars and lorries, and there's little in the way of signals and

An itinerant mohinga *seller in Mandalay reading on his break.* Mohinga *is Burma's national dish — a fish noodle soup that comes with all sorts of accompaniments including the split pea crackers you can see hanging in the pink plastic bag.*

One of the many noodle stalls in Mandalay's central Zegyo market.

road-markings, so crossing the street means holding your breath, walking straight into traffic and hoping for the best. But the dry heat of Mandalay means that the pace of life is slow, so casualties are (relatively) rare.

And as for the street food – every day, my six-foot four-inch *Po Po* would sit in his huge wicker chair in the open garage at the side of the house, so he could watch life go by and, more importantly, flag down every passing snack-seller. I'd be dancing around in the living room with the radio blaring, only to be interrupted constantly by my parents yelling, 'Shan noodles are here!', 'There's coconut sago pudding!', 'Come and get some pickled *mayan-thi* [green marian plum]!'

The last of those visitors was the most entertaining to me as a child, as the pickle vendor would herald his arrival by beating a small gong, which to a Burmese ear sounds like '*naun! naun!*'. As a result, such vendors are called *naun naun thair* i.e. 'the bong bong sellers'.

> No! you won't 'eed nothin' else
> But them spicy garlic smells,
> An' the sunshine an' the palm-trees an' the
> tinkly temple-bells;
> On the road to Mandalay
>
> Rudyard Kipling, *The Road to Mandalay*

In the rare event of no vendors choosing to pass by that day, there was a *mont-yay-bar* rice pancake seller who sizzled her dishes to order just in front of the house, sending seductive aromas of frying onion and garlic our way. Around the corner was a tiny night market (*nya zay dan*), which touted all manner of fantastic snacks such as *mont lin mayar* – crispy little shells of batter stuffed with boiled peas, shredded spring onions, the occasional chunk of tomato and quivering quail eggs.

And in every other direction as far as the eye could see, there were more roadside stalls with their own irresistible specialities. I remember watching *The Burma Road* at the age of nine back in England, when I spied the presenter Miles Kington eating *Mandalay mont-di* noodles – a delectable 'salad' of fat, blowsy rice noodles, chicken curry, chillies, coriander and sharp, sliced raw onions. In raptures, I jumped up and shrieked to my mother, 'I know that stall! I've been to that stall! It's right next to *Po Po* and *Pwa Pwa*'s house!'

Even now, although my grandparents have since passed away, the pancake seller is still in front of the house driving everyone wild with the scent of sizzling onions; the street vendors continue to strut past daily with their panniers of plenty; and that night market still bustles away, surrounded by crowds satisfying their snacky cravings.

The only difference is that these days we catch a plane from Yangon to Mandalay. The railway romanticism is lost, but our eager stomachs are filled that much sooner. Mandalay International Airport is about an hour's drive from Mandalay proper – 'international' being a mildly amusing misnomer as the only planes to fly into this white elephant come from within Burma itself, apart from the occasional flight from Kunming, China. The actual road to Mandalay is an absolute joy – noisy, dusty, beautiful and bumpy with all manner of picturesque traffic, like sidecar rickshaws, vintage mopeds and genuine beasts of burden.

Our first port of call nowadays is an Indian tea shop called *Pan Thakin* (Flower Lord), where we hunker down on tiny wooden stools to be served one of the finest breakfasts known to man – a metal platter of *aloo poori*. First thing in the morning, nothing beats dunking huge, crispy, freshly fried puffy breads in curried potatoes and spicy tamarind sauce. On the side, there are samosas to snack on, shredded cabbage and onion chunks to crunch, lime to squeeze and fresh chillies and mint leaves to nibble.

My father plumps for his favourite dish of *samusa thoke* – samosa salad, about which the great writer and chef Madhur Jaffrey had this to say:

> One of the most unusual Burmese-Indian creations in the market is a samosa salad. Two very Indian snacks, deep-fried, savoury pastries and split pea fritters, along with boiled potatoes and tomatoes, are crumbled and dressed with lime juice, as well as a sauce made with dal, rather like a thin, south Indian sambar.
>
> Madhur Jaffrey, *Ultimate Curry Bible*, 2003

And when I'm back in cold and blustery Blighty, especially in the depths of winter, I would give anything to be back on that roadside, sipping cups of hot green tea and chewing on sprigs of mint. I love Yangon with all my heart, yet it's not until I'm in Mandalay that I feel that I've truly come home.

Land of Rubies

My mother's family is from Mogok, a gem-mining town bordering the Shan State. In contrast to sultry Mandalay, Mogok is definitely a hill town with chilly weather to match – it even used to snow there when my mother was a child.

Mogok is also remarkable for the fact that it's where 90 per cent of the world's rubies come from. My mother's mother, Daw Aye, managed a small gem mine and her father, U Thein Pe, was a gem-cutter, and in fact, my great, great-grandfather was U Hmat, known as the Ruby King of Burma, who famously traded in precious gemstones in the late 1800s, and was even rumoured to have been knighted by Queen Victoria in absentia.

U Hmat (1841–1916), my great, great-grandfather, who lived in Mogok near the Shan State and was known as the Ruby King. He was the chief ruby miner to King Thibaw, the last king of Burma.

U Hmat was great here in the days before any Englishman had come within sight of Mogok. He is not a foreigner … but a native of the soil. He lives some distance from the market place in a rambling wooden house on piles… At one end he has built himself a strong room of brick, in which lie hidden, according to popular tradition, rubies of extraordinary value.

U Hmat is seldom seen abroad. He goes, it is said, in terror of his life; and his courtyard is thronged with retainers, who make for him a kind of personal bodyguard. But in bygone days he travelled every year to Mandalay with a present of rubies, and was received in audience by the king.

He is a builder of many monasteries and pagodas; but is said to be less lavish in this respect than most of his compatriots in Burma. He is believed accordingly by his European neighbours to have 'his head screwed on the right way.' His character for economy is the topic of very favourable discussion at the dinner tables of the settlement, and it is a commonplace of opinion that he is the only Burman at the mines who is not a fool.

Let it be added that he is the father of a pretty daughter, whose jewels are the despair of every other woman in Mogok, and that he keeps her in strict seclusion, lest some adventurous youth should steal away her heart, or her person, or both. He has been good enough, however, to show me some of her most beautiful jewels.

V.C. Scott O'Connor, *The Silken East*, 1905

Much to my family's sadness, the money has long since gone, but until recently one of my uncles still had a few shares in a ruby mine – we visited him there one year, and I remember seeing a big whiteboard with a list of the biggest gems and their mind-blowing sale prices. I also remember seeing a bowl full of unpolished rubies and I briefly considered pocketing a couple (in *The Dark Knight Returns*, the butler Alfred tells an anecdote about coming across a boy in Burma who was 'playing with a ruby the size of a tangerine' and that isn't too far from the truth).

Although most of my mother's family eventually moved down to Yangon, her two brothers decided to stay in their childhood home, and divided it into two for their own families. And so, we would undertake a six-hour journey by pick-up truck from Mandalay to Mogok up a narrow, winding mountain path to visit them.

The route to the top was made all the more treacherous by the fact that, insanely, it was open to two-way traffic, so our precarious progress was constantly punctuated by a honking horn to warn any unwary on-comers.

Halfway up the mountain, we'd always pause at a little village called Shwenyaungbin (Golden Banyan) to stretch our legs and for the driver to have a well-earned rest. The smouldering smell of wood burning marked this recognised truck stop, where we would draw our tiny stools closer to the fire to ward off the chill and indulge in *kya zan hin*, an intense, smoky broth packed with sweet, charred dried shrimp, earthy wood-ear mushrooms and slippery bean thread noodles. With a sprinkle of roasted chilli, a dash of fish sauce and a squeeze of lime, every spoonful warmed us and dazzled our taste buds.

We'd also stuff ourselves with fried slices of potato, piping hot from the wok (similar to 'potato scallops' and so much better than chips), and steamed tubes of bamboo crammed with sticky rice, which we would open immediately, risking third-degree burns to get to the fragrant goodness inside.

This feast was always followed by mugs of hot, sugary, milk-powdery coffee (an instant type known as 3-in-1 in Burma) and thick slabs of *mont-gyut*, a kind of sweet, biscuity bread similar to shop-bought French toast. Forget motorway service stations – this was the way to break your journey in style. As we watched the embers crackle and glow, we felt happy and snug and replete.

And when we eventually got to the top, we'd be greeted with open arms and hot water bottles. Extremities dealt with, we'd warm up our insides with dish after dish of pork – stewed, braised, fried, roasted, steamed and even pickled. Never mind rubies – in Mogok, pork was king, and every little bit was used, head to tail and everything in between. So valued was this meat in my mother's birthplace, that the Mogok slang for wages was *wet-thar bo* (literally 'pork funds') and people would say cheerily, 'I'm off to earn today's pork funds now' – a bit like 'bringing home the bacon'.

One of my favourite Mogok snacks is still *wet-ooh-chauk* – pig intestines that have been seasoned and hung up to dry like salami and then cut into chunks, salted, and stir-fried until crunchy and crisp. And whilst they went beautifully with a plate of steamed rice and some garlicky greens at suppertime, I would make sure to squirrel away a salty bowlful to snack on like the finest pork scratchings whilst gossiping with my cousins and drinking green tea.

The next day, while the world was still misty, we'd have cold showers we poured ourselves from a tank, and I'd insist that my mother also boiled a kettle of water for me, for which I was deemed a big wuss. Then my uncle would take us for a stroll to the nearby Shan market where we'd buy, yes, more pork, but also vegetables and other ingredients for the day from the cheerful stallholders. We would eat Shan tofu and Shan noodles, and try to peek discreetly at all the tribespeople who had also come to town, both to buy and to sell.

With my father's family at Upali Thein Ordination Hall in Nyaung-U. I'm the one in the multi-coloured dress, my big brothers are behind me.

On the road with both sides of the family. My grandmother is in the black cardigan and I'm the one in the white dress.

Then my cousin, my uncle's daughter, would appear on her Vespa, somehow elegantly dressed in a denim jacket, *htamein* (sarong), flip-flops and a vintage Army helmet. She'd offer to take me for a ride and we would whizz around the narrow streets and weave between the red-roofed houses whilst enjoying the cool breeze.

The sad thing about Mogok being the land of rubies is that 'foreigners' aren't allowed to visit unless they have 'legitimate business', which in practice means gem trading. My husband, a pesky foreigner, has applied to visit on numerous occasions, but no matter how much we vouch for him, each time he has been turned down at the last minute. I couldn't go without him, especially now we have children, so until things change (and I do hope they will), I won't be able to return. I miss Mogok very much, but it's becoming more of a distant dream as time passes.

Travelling around Burma

My parents are both doctors and before they moved to the UK, they had become well used to being posted by the Burmese equivalent of the NHS all around the country, and they greatly enjoyed exploring the different regions and trying local cuisines. When they returned, a yen to discover more of Burma beyond the familial hubs of Yangon, Mandalay and Mogok remained within them, and my brothers and I were more than happy to benefit from their wanderlust.

Thus, they would hire a minibus and/or flat-bed truck and take us (and various family members who would invariably tag along) to Bagan, the land of ancient pagodas; to Inle, birthplace of my maternal grandfather, famous for its tranquil lake, its leg-rowers and the freshest fish imaginable; and to the old colonial town of Maymyo (now known as Pyin Oo Lwin), with its horse-drawn carriages, stunning botanical gardens and the sweetest little strawberries.

We'd travel to Mount Popa, the home of the spirits we call *nats*, as well as less spiritual, more menacing, macaques who we'd distract with juicy mangoes; to the hill-tribe towns of Taunggyi and Pindaya in the Shan State, full of folk haggling in the thriving fruit and vegetable markets; and to Kyaikto in the Mon State, gnawing on sugarcane to sustain us as we made our slow pilgrimage to lofty Kyaiktiyo, the Golden Rock Pagoda allegedly shaped like the Buddha's head.

And everywhere we went in Burma, we'd feast on the local cuisine and pester the stallholders and chefs to give away their secrets on how to make the lushest pork and rice noodles or the crispiest gourd fritters. Sometimes, if we were lucky, they'd even oblige. It never felt cheeky to ask them – it was sort of like exploring my heritage – as like many Burmese natives, I'm an ethnic mix (of Shan, Bamar, Yunnanese and Intha – there are in fact over 130 different ethnic groups that make up the country).

Back in Blighty

My mother is known as the best cook around by friends and family in Burma as well as the Burmese community here, and, not one to rest on her laurels, she'd take the hints and tips gleaned from our many excursions and fold them into her already extensive culinary knowledge.

Where ingredients were impossible to track down back in England, my mother would happily experiment with alternatives until she found a substitute that gained our hearty approval – for example, leafy spinach instead of *gazun-ywet* (water spinach), or durum wheat spaghetti instead of *mont-di bat* (round rice noodles). But certain foodstuffs like *lahpet* (pickled tea) were completely irreplaceable, so several times a year our family would make the trip to the Port of Tilbury, just outside of London, and climb aboard a ship manned by Burmese sailors who brought priceless provisions from back home. I still remember going to use their loo at the age of six, and being bemused by a calendar pinned to the door that showed ladies in various states of undress.

My mother never once gave my brothers and me 'kids' food' – just less spicy versions of what she and my father ate, so my love for Burmese cuisine was established from an early age. In anticipation of every meal, I'd hang around my mother as she bustled around the kitchen, and I'd absorb the sights and smells like a sponge, whilst trying to quiet my rumbling belly. I'd watch her chop crispy roast pork and duck into glossy lacquered chunks with her big cleaver to pile over gravied rice with caramelised onions, or shred green beans and mushrooms and stir-fry them with garlic and ginger until mouth-wateringly fragrant, and there was nowhere else I would rather have been.

Although the kitchen was definitely her domain, my mother would let me assist a little here and there, as she knew that I was dying to join in with her creations. To this day, my favourite dish is *Mandalay meeshay* (a spicy, garlicky, zingy wonder of a noodle dish) and it was my extra-special job to pound the yellow bean sauce into a fine paste – in fact there's even a photo of me doing this with gusto at the tender age of four. It was only at university that I realised that this task was completely redundant and simply my mother's way of making me feel like I was being useful.

Like many mothers around the world, feeding us was how my mother expressed her love, and this need to nourish has definitely and inevitably passed on to me. This is a huge part of why I wanted to share Burmese food with the rest of the world, first via my blog, *meemalee's kitchen*, then via my online

My paternal great-grandfather U Htin's recipe for condensed milk, typed out on his old typewriter. Note the use of 'ticals' — Burma is one of only three countries that have not adopted the metric system as their official system of weights and measures (the others being the USA and Liberia). Partly based on the Pali system, Burmese weights and measures are worth looking up, as they are as confusing as they are poetic.

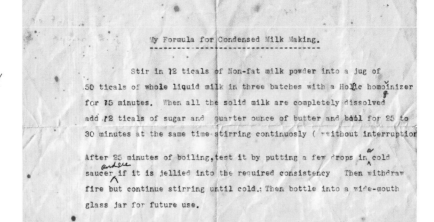

My Formula for Condensed Milk Making.

Stir in 12 ticals of Non-fat milk powder into a jug of 50 ticals of whole liquid milk in three batches with a Hollic homoinizer for 15 minutes. When all the solid milk are completely dissolved add 12 ticals of sugar and quarter ounce of butter and boil for 25 to 30 minutes at the same time stirring continuosly (without interruption

After 25 minutes of boiling, test it by putting a few drops in cold saucer and see if it is jellied into the required consistency Then withdraw fire but continue stirring until cold. Then bottle into a wide-mouth glass jar for future use.

Three sisters: from left to right, my great-aunt and famous writer and dissident 'Ludu' Daw Amar; my paternal grandmother Daw Tin Tin; and my great-aunt and cheroot tycoon 'Naga' Daw Oo. Their fourth sister (the baby, Daw Kyin) and two brothers are not pictured. My grandmother originally had a paper, printing ink and stationery supplies shop called the Burmese Paper Mart and, as a senior member of the Upper Burma Chamber of Commerce, she was part of the welcome party for China's Prime Minister Zhou Enlai on one of his visits to Burma. Later on, she started a printing press called Daw Tin Tin & Sons Press which printed my Pwa Oo's Naga brand cheroot labels and supplied materials for my Pwa Amar's publications, including her newspaper The Ludu Daily.

community, Burmese Food and Beyond, and now by writing this book – that, and the fact that I want to show you all how fantastic Burmese food is.

With Great Culinary Power Comes Great Responsibility

To people who come to Burma for the first time there are two things about the status of our women that seem to impress them with particular force. My foreign friends have often told me that they are surprised to see an ordinary Burmese woman sitting at her stall in a bazaar, dressed in the usual *htamein* and jacket, her hair arranged on top of her head in the traditional manner, often smoking a cigar – and handling her trade with all the hard-headed business acumen of a man. Or, in an agricultural family, the wife may be helping with the planting, the reaping, the winnowing. If her husband is a cartman, a Burmese woman may perform her share of the labour. You can see her in business houses, signing contracts and making decisions for the firm, or find her in any of the professions or in parliament. It all seems quite different from the familiar picture of the downtrodden, backward Asian woman.

Daw Mya Sein, 'The Women of Burma', *The Atlantic,* February, 1958

Burma is the largest Tibeto-Burman polity on the planet, and matriarchal and matrilineal societies are so common in Tibeto-Burman culture that one could argue they are the norm. Certainly, on a domestic and cultural level, Burmese women are in charge. We have no surnames and we keep our property, and if we marry, although husbands may be the 'rice winners', it's the wives who control the finances, giving spending money to their other halves.

One of the other reasons that women rule the roost is our food. The Burmese are completely led by their stomachs – so much so that we ask friends and family if they've eaten before bothering to ask how they are – '*Htamin sar bee-bee lar*?' literally means, 'Have you had your rice yet?'. In fact, this is how we say hello – the greeting '*Mingalaba*' was invented by the Burmese government in the 1960s to mimic the 'Good Morning' used in missionary schools, and most Burmese people don't actually use it with each other.

Recipes are therefore considered powerful and treated as a closely guarded secret, handed down from mother to daughter (or niece). An aunt of mine once foolishly disclosed her recipe for Shan tofu to her housekeeper, who then, much to my aunt's chagrin, promptly scarpered to set up a tofu business back in her own village.

Yet here I am willing to share these secrets with you all – I adore Burmese food and I feel compelled to spread the love. My mother hasn't disowned me just yet, so you should make the most of it whilst you can.

I can't wait to introduce you all to this multitude of flavours, scents, colours and textures. We eat with all of our senses, and with Burmese food you can indulge each and every one of them – the aroma from a bubbling pot of cinnamon chicken, the multicoloured vision of a salad of papaya, carrots and coriander, the sensation of rice noodles silky with sauce, or the crunch of a handful of homemade split pea crackers.

I hope you enjoy Burmese food, and making it, as much as I do.

With love,

MiMi Aye
London, 2019

Vegetables at a local market including tiny green mangoes, fresh jujubes and sprouting djenkol beans.

Daikon seller at Kaingdan Market, Mandalay. Kaingdan is the largest retail and wholesale market for fresh produce near Zegyo, the central market in Mandalay.

The Food of Burma

So, what exactly is Burmese food? People constantly ask me to summarise, but it's difficult to distil into a few words. Moreover, before we get any further, you need to know that Burma is made up of over 130 ethnic groups, and the food that I know, cook and grew up with is from the Bamar and the Shan, who make up around three-quarters of the population. I suspect that all the other groups and cuisines deserve culinary tomes of their own.

Bearing in mind the disclaimer that *Mandalay* covers mainstream Burmese food, let's start with what you won't find. Like many South East Asian countries, dairy isn't a big deal in Burma. A number of factors are involved: little pastoral land, a historical lack of refrigeration and a respect for cattle in agriculture – milk is considered to be for the calves; cows and bulls are part of a Burmese farmer's family.

In fact, for a long time I never realised that, although scarce and extremely expensive, milk and butter *was* actually available. Until 20 or so years ago, there were no supermarkets in Burma (see also page 38), and food was always bought daily – fresh from open-air markets and so early in the morning I was usually still in bed.

We even used to pack Lurpak butter in our suitcase to take all the way to my grandparents in Mandalay – frozen and quadruple-wrapped in aluminium foil along with a tub of Brylcreem, a parcel of fruit cake and countless bars of Dairy Milk (my grandparents have since passed away, but we still take chocolate for the rest of the family every time we go home).

Most of the Burmese world preferred those 3-in-1 packet mixes with coffee, creamer and sugar combined rather than fresh milk, and prior to that they would have added a fat dollop of condensed milk to get the desired level of milky sweetness.

There's still a huge condensed milk factory in Maymyo, just beyond Mandalay – condensed milk (known as *note-zee*) was used in Burma to make ice cream and Indian sweets and puddings, and at least one of my other cousins was known to squeeze it neat into her mouth as sometimes it came in tubes rather than tins.

Such was the desire for condensed milk, it even cropped up in savoury recipes – for example in Coconut Chicken Noodles (page 109), partly in the wrong-headed belief that it was somehow much healthier than coconut milk.

Talking of coconut milk, one of my particular bugbears is the misconception in some circles that Burmese food is all about coconuts. That dish of coconut chicken noodles, mentioned earlier, is a relative newcomer to Burma despite its popularity and even renown abroad as a cousin to Thailand's *khao soi*. It came from Lower Burma and was first found in coastal Mawlamyine – it's similar to laksa, so I suspect it must have come from laksa country, e.g. Malaysia or Singapore. The dish arrived in Yangon, post-war, but didn't reach Mandalay until the 1960s, and it got to the Shan State even later than that.

At any rate, coconuts are only grown on the coast in Burma. They're traditionally feared as a contributor to hypertension – in fact, evaporated and/or condensed milk is often preferred as a 'healthy' substitute for coconut milk. As a result, coconuts are only used in Burmese desserts (most of which have been pinched from other countries), those coconut chicken noodles and *ohn htamin* (coconut rice, which again probably came from elsewhere).

Because they're relatively uncommon and considered a treat, fresh green coconuts are prized as offerings to *nats* (our animist spirits), monasteries and pagodas, and they're essential for *shinbyu* ceremonies. *Shinbyu* is, I guess, the Burmese Buddhist equivalent of the Jewish *bar mitzvah*, where boys and young men are celebrated as princes, much like the Buddha, before spending a short while as novice monks.

So, with all of those caveats, Burmese food is a little like Thai food and a little like Indian food and a little like Chinese food, and such influences are hardly surprising since those are the neighbouring countries. But the cuisine takes these elements and combines them with local techniques, ingredients and flavours to make something delicious and unique, as well as having a fair few curveballs of its own (for example, our fabled pickled tea, page 31, or infamous lemon salad, page 64).

Subtlety is often the key to Burmese cuisine – no crude hit of chilli or one-dimensional note of sweetness – every dish has at least three of the five tastes of salty, sweet, sour, bitter and umami, and every meal has a host of accompaniments. Variety really is the spice of life for the Burmese palate. Though with regard to spice, we're obsessed with condiments, and it's standard practice to season a dish ourselves just before we dig in. For example, the national breakfast of *mohinga* (Fish Noodle Soup, page 106) comes with fish sauce, chilli oil and lime wedges to add to your liking at the table. Or we'll scatter crispy fried onions and drizzle toasted groundnut oil on a soup before we take our first sip.

It's also important to know that we adore texture almost as much as flavour. Burmese Tofu Fritters (page 44) are a brilliant

Fried chicken vendors flock to our car window on the way to Mount Popa. They seem to magically appear during every road trip, and I like to call them The Chicken Ladies (sung to the Beyoncé tune). (See page 148 for my BFC recipe.)

Various types of dried fish, eel and shrimp at Mingala Market, Mandalay.

showcase for both of these attributes – they're crisp on the outside, soft and meltingly fluffy on the inside and so tasty that any dipping sauce serves to enhance rather than disguise (funnily enough, they are quite similar to a Sicilian snack known as *panelle*). Although it should be said that fritters are huge in Burma full stop – I joke that we will deep-fry anything that doesn't move and some things that do – and markets are packed with fritter vendors luring you in like wok-wielding sirens with their irresistible sights and smells. These fried snacks always come with a sharp dipping sauce to cut through any grease, not that there's much fear of either as they're usually eaten fresh from the wok. The catch-all term for this dip is *tchin-ngan-zat*, literally 'sour, salty, spicy', which is a popular triumvirate for the Burmese palate.

My favourite dish *Mandalay meeshay* (page 44) is another good example of how the Burmese satisfy our craving for texture as much as flavour. It's sour, sweet, savoury, salty and garlicky, and features soft yet toothsome noodles, crunchy sour pickles, bean sprouts that snap to the bite, and rich, tender chunks of pork.

Unsurprisingly, noodles are a mainstay in Burma, made of wheat, rice, egg and mung bean, but they're often considered a snack rather than a proper meal. It's a plate of rice that we want at the end of the day (or the start or the middle), and it's rice that gives the Burmese strength. Burma was once known as the rice bowl of Asia, and it is still the world's sixth largest producer of rice. *Paw hsan hmwe* is the most popular rice in Burma and a day-to-day meal resembles the Indonesian *rijsttafel* or Thai *khantok*, where a vast array of dishes serves only to enhance the star that is steamed rice.

And what goes with that beautiful rice? The great Irrawaddy River flows right through Burma, which means freshwater fish and shrimp are a mainstay everywhere, used in a variety of ways: fresh, salted and dried whole or in fillets (often in elaborate fan shapes), pickled, or pounded to a paste with salt and then left to ferment in the sun.

The pounded, fermented version is known as *ngapi* (page 260), which literally means 'fish pressed', although it can be made of whole fish, small fry, sometimes shrimp or a mix. Similar to shrimp paste, it is so prevalent in Burma (particularly Lower Burma) both as a condiment and as an ingredient that it encompasses most of Burmese cuisine. It's said that you can never be Burmese if you don't love *ngapi*, and the joke goes that it 'runs through our veins'. Those with rural accents are even teased for having a *ngapi* twang to their voice.

So what's *ngapi* like? It bears some resemblance to Gentleman's Relish aka *Patum Peperium*, but it's used as a magic ingredient to transform something ordinary into something wondrous. It's salty and packed with umami – think fish sauce with rocket boosters. *Ngapi* can be fried up into an oily sambal known as *ngapi kyaw* (page 211). It can be cooked into a curry, known as *ngapi chet* (page 208), a classic from Mandalay. It's simmered into a sauce for rice and vegetables known as *ngapi yay-kyo* (page 204), essential in a Yangon household. It goes into my favourite condiment known as *ngapi htaung* (page 207). A pinch of *ngapi* is often thrown into any savoury dish in the same way that salt is used in the West and soy sauce in the rest of Asia. However, the Shan notably do not use *ngapi*, and instead prefer to use fermented soybeans known as *pe pote* (page 241) in a similar way. Also note that yellow bean sauce is known as *pe ngapi* in Burma i.e. 'bean *ngapi*', as in some recipes it is interchangeable.

So, most of Burma thrives on freshwater fish and shrimp. However, seafood such as crab and lobster has only really been common in coastal areas such as Sittwe, Mawlamyine and Dawei as historically, movement in Burma has been restricted, and cross-country transport connections have been poor. This enforced localisation has, however, led to two interesting developments. Firstly, our tastes have evolved according to the produce available, so that *wet gaung thoke* (pig's head salad) would be made with onions in Mandalay, but in Yangon, the same dish would be made using cucumber instead, or at the end of a meal in Mandalay, you'd be served wedges of fresh pineapple, whereas in Yangon, you'd be treated to some sliced watermelon. Secondly, necessity has been the mother of engaging invention – recipes tend to use the same handful of ingredients but in different ways, sometimes within the same dish – e.g. you'll get *htamin chin* (Shan sour rice) that's made with fresh garlic, crispy fried garlic and garlic oil.

Beef isn't that popular in Burma, mainly because of the belief I mentioned earlier that cows and bulls are part of a Burmese farmer's family. Goat is preferred to lamb, which s relatively rare – when we say mutton, we're referring to goat. Pork though is regarded with near reverence, for its versatility as well as its flavour– and not just in my mother's hometown of Mogok. Weirdly, chicken has historically been the most expensive meat in Burma. It's usually scrawny, resembling its ancestor the jungle fowl, but always bursting with flavour, and is the second-most loved meat after pork. The Burmese tend to reject breast as being too dry and pappy, and will head straight for the wing, thigh or drumstick, as well as the neckbone, heart and gizzard.

Very few people in Burma are strict vegetarians, so where meat is not on the menu, it's often a result of privation and/or because of superstition or religious observance, e.g. those that believe in the animist spirits called *nats* may shun pork and those told by their astrologer not to eat chicken on a Friday will adhere to this, sometimes maddeningly so. Veganism is even rarer, as eggs are a particular favourite. They deliver a kind of punch that a carrot won't, being packed with umami. They're extremely versatile as well, and can be employed in

This street food
vendor in Mandalay
sells various sweet
snacks made from
glutinous rice and
coconut. After she
serves you, she
wraps everything up
and then balances it
on the bamboo tray
on her head as she
walks along.

Green vegetables
at Yankin Backstreet
Market, Yangon.
Note the green
mangoes at the
front that have been
pickled and then cut
into intricate spirals.

Burmese soups, stir-fries, salads and even curries. Duck eggs (*be u*) are more common than hens' eggs (*kyet u*) in Burma, since more ducks are kept than chickens, and this happy situation means that the sunniest yolks end up in the pot. Quail eggs (*ngon u*) are practically ten a penny and are often bought off the street and eaten as a casual snack, hard-boiled and dipped in a little salt. Note that we would never say *u* ('egg') by itself, because the failure to specify an egg's provenance sounds odd and slightly disturbing to the Burmese ear.

Talking of disturbing, such is our love for certain foods, we have no qualms about eating those that endanger our health. A favourite Burmese snack is boiled *danyinthee* (djenkol bean) dipped in oil and salt, which when eaten in excessive quantities will cause renal failure (look up djenkolism), but even this doesn't stop gluttons from getting carried away. High cholesterol is also a problem in Burma due to our love of fat and oil, but when statins are prescribed to combat it, those afflicted will slyly continue to eat pomelo even though this will aggravate the side effects of their medication. As for high blood pressure caused by our addiction to salty food – the less said about that, the better.

Until relatively recently, diabetes has been less of a problem because desserts after dinner have never been a thing. Most Burmese puddings are enjoyed as snacks and seem to have arrived from elsewhere in the world e.g. *falooda* and semolina cake being of Indian origin (pages 229 and 221) and coconut marble jelly from Thailand (page 222). I suspect Malaysia was the provenance for our beloved *Shwe Yin Aye* (page 225) and even the floating rice balls eaten at New Year (page 226). We're also big fans of Indian sweets such as *nankhatai*, *jalebi*, *rasmalai* and *gulab jamun*.

I still think the best way to indulge a sweet tooth is with wonderful fresh produce, and many in Burma would agree – the juiciest watermelon from Yangon, the finest pomelo from Mawlamyine, the ripest oranges and pineapple from the Shan State, the sweetest little strawberries from Maymyo and the best melon and jackfruit from Mandalay. The king of all Burmese fruits is the mango, grown in Mandalay, Kyaukse and Pyin Oo Lwin, with the most exquisite variety being the fragrant *sein ta lone* mango, meaning 'diamond solitaire'.

We're just as fond of pickled and preserved fruits, which are definitely more sour than sweet – think Asiatic gooseberries and plums, starfruit and jujubes, flowering quinces and ambarellas (the last two having the hilarious names in Burmese of *chin-saw-gar thee* – 'insultingly sour fruit' – and *gwei thee* – 'testicle fruit'). The fresh versions of these same fruits are even popular as a savoury snack, dipped into a mixture of salt, liquorice powder and chilli powder known as *thone-myo-sut* (literally 'three kinds blended'). We even eat fruit while they're still unripe. Green tomatoes and papaya go into salads, and slices of baby mango will be dunked in *ngapi*.

However, in Burma, the most treasured food of all is oil. One thing that is mentioned time and again in guidebooks to Burma is the fact that many of our curries are quite oily. There are a number of reasons for this. An abundance of oil is a sign of generosity as the best (groundnut) oil is very expensive. It's a good way of keeping the food from spoiling. And it's also because we're just really keen on oil. In the same way the biggest insult to a baker would be to say their cake was dry, the hugest slap to a Burmese chef would be to say of their dish, '*si nair de*' – 'it lacks oil'. There's even a Burmese proverb that goes: 'With a helping of oil, one could even eat straw.'

A happy fritter-seller in Mandalay. Her cheeks are painted with thanaka, a fragrant paste made from ground wood which is universally worn throughout Burma and one of the first things most visitors notice. Thanaka is used as make-up, sunblock and medicine, as it is thought to treat acne, soothe itches and reduce scars. Traditionally the thanaka bark is ground to a paste on a circular stone slab known as a kyauk-pyin, but these days you can also get thanaka in a ready-to-use block form (just add water) and even a cream. When my paternal grandmother passed away, my aunt gave me her kyauk-pyin and it's one of my most treasured possessions.

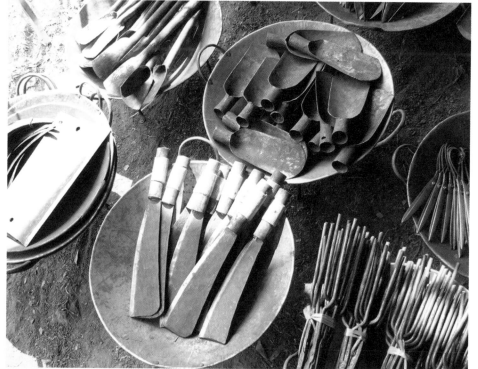

Various tools for sale near Shwe Sar Yan Pagoda by the River Myitnge. From left to right: cleaver blades, trowel and spade heads, machetes, charcoal tongs and kitchen scissors. Even now, the machete is a Burmese farmer's primary implement, but when my parents were growing up, every household, town or country, would have had a machete, as it was used for splitting bamboo and sugar cane and chopping firewood and meat. Machetes are also used to cut toddy palm stems to get sap for making jaggery and palm wine. My mother still uses hers to trim her rosebushes, much to her neighbours' consternation.

Eating & Serving Customs

In days of yore, the Burmese would eat all their meals at a low round wooden table, while sitting cross-legged (for men and children) or kneeling with one's feet tucked to one side (for women) on a bamboo mat on the floor. Whilst this is still the case in the countryside where life is somewhat more traditional, standard dining tables and chairs have taken over in the rest of Burma, but in fact, many Burmese people still sit at them with their knees bent and feet up on the seat because apparently it's more comfortable.

What we eat has barely changed, however. Even the most basic meal will comprise a spread of steamed rice with *hin* i.e. curries (for want of a better word – these are sauced dishes of fish, meat or poultry), a vegetable dish and a broth called *hin-gyo* or, if sour, *chin-yay hin*. Also on offer are sour, salty or spicy condiments such as the ubiquitous fermented fish dip known as *ngapi yay-kyo* or the pungent and oily *balachaung* (*ngapi kyaw*) with crudites or blanched vegetables, and green fruits such as baby mangoes to dunk, which also add zing to every meal. Finally, there might be hot fried foods to savour on the side, such as gourd fritters or even prawn crackers.

How we eat hasn't really changed either. There are no courses, and dishes are served at the same time. Before everyone dives in, the most senior diners (in terms of age or prestige) are served first. And even when there are no elders present, a spoonful of rice will be scooped out from the pot and put aside as an act of respect, a custom known as *u cha* (literally, 'first serve'). I still do this every day at home – I think my (English) husband thinks I'm slightly barmy, but he doesn't dare question me.

As for the utensils – well, for the main part, none are necessary because traditionally the Burmese eat with their hands. The method is as follows:

1. Shape some rice into a small ball with just the fingertips of your right hand;
2. Mix the rice with whatever tempting titbits you fancy;
3. Turn your hand over so your fingers form a kind of upwards scoop;
4. Push the rice ball into your mouth with your thumb.

With a little practice, it's pretty easy and even elegant (the food shouldn't go past your knuckles, and certainly not onto your palms), and my husband is an old pro now.

We do use cutlery for noodle dishes – chopsticks for some of them, metal Chinese/Thai spoons for others. Although to be honest, noodle salads are more likely to be eaten by hand, meaning you can really tuck in with gusto. Knives are rare, but some Burmese people do use a fork and spoon at all times (they think it's modern to do so). Forks and spoons are always provided in restaurants, but I (and most of my family) find this akin to eating burgers with a knife and fork – ungainly, unsatisfying and just a little bit pretentious.

Note that drinks are not served during the meal. Instead, liquid refreshment comes as a broth or soup, which is served from a communal bowl. You can either drizzle this onto your rice (though some people, like one of my brothers, like to drown their rice in soup, a method called *yay baw-law*) or you can sup it delicately from a spoon between bites.

Since all the food is served at once, there are two ways that generally signal the end of a meal, other than plates being scraped clean by enthusiastic diners. In either case, green tea will be served alongside, which we call *yay nway gyan* – literally meaning 'rough hot water'.

The first way is with a dish or pot of *htanyet* – a golden jaggery made from toddy palm syrup that comes in bite-size pieces and is sometimes referred to 'Burmese chocolate'. This is the closest thing that we have to a formal dessert, as sweetmeats are usually considered snacks or a mid-morning or afternoon treat. Occasionally a piece of fruit may be provided as well.

The second way is the appearance of *lahpet* (pickled tea) – a bittersweet, astringent and savoury food that's unique to Burma. If *mohinga* is Burma's national dish, *lahpet* is our pride and joy. Burmese writer U Ba Than said that without the presence of *lahpet*, 'no party nor feast, nor even a formal festivity is complete'. It's so beloved that there is even a rhyming proverb that goes:

A-thee mar, thayet; a-thar mar, wet; a-ywet mar, lahpet.

roughly translated as:

Of all the fruit, mango's the best;
Of all the meat, pork's the best;
And of all the leaves, lahpet's the best.

Lahpet has huge cultural, religious and political significance in Burma. It was an ancient symbolic peace offering between opposing kingdoms: it was literally used to end wars. In pre-colonial and colonial times, *lahpet* would be served after a

A collection of Burman and Shan hsun-ok belonging to my mother and me. Hsun-ok are vessels used to present offerings to the Buddha and the sangha, the community of monks. They are traditionally placed on an altar either side of a Buddha image, and gifts of flowers, fruit and incense are placed inside them. Hsun-ok are very light as they are usually made of bamboo and lacquer and decorated with coloured glass and gold leaf. However, the small one in the foreground was carved out of wood by my paternal grandfather in the 1950s.

judge made a verdict, and if the arbitrators ate it, this conveyed their formal acceptance.

There are two main styles of *lahpet* – *a-hlu lahpet* (meaning 'almsgiving or donation ceremony lahpet') also known as Mandalay *lahpet*, and *lahpet thoke* (meaning 'lahpet salad') also known as Yangon *lahpet*.

A-hlu lahpet or Mandalay *lahpet* is served in a divided lacquerware dish called a *lahpet ohk*, which is covered with a lid when not in use. The pickled tea leaves, dressed with groundnut oil or sesame oil, are placed in the middle and surrounded by a whole host of garnishes including crispy fried garlic, crispy fried hyacinth beans, roasted chana dal, toasted sesame seeds, fried red-skin peanuts, dried shrimp, pickled ginger shreds and occasionally fried shredded coconut. It's eaten by taking a little *lahpet* with a spoon or your fingertips and mixing it with a different combination of garnishes each time, so that each mouthful is different.

A-hlu lahpet appears at all weddings (it was served at mine) and at *soon-kyway*, a ceremonial offering of food to Buddhist monks. Guests are invited to a *shinbyu* (a Buddhist rite-of-passage akin to a *bar mitzvah*) by the host knocking on their doors with a *lahpet ohk*, and one accepts by taking a bite. It's even left as offerings to *nats*, the guardian spirits of forests, mountains, rivers and fields, who we revered long before the Buddha came onto the scene.

This form of *lahpet* isn't reserved for special occasions though – every household will have a *lahpet ohk*, which they keep topped up and it will be brought out for (unexpected) visitors with a pot of green tea, in the same way you might offer guests some biscuits or cake with their tea or coffee.

The second type, *lahpet thoke* or Yangon *lahpet* is prepared by mixing everything that appears in the *lahpet ohk* with sliced tomatoes, fresh garlic and green chilli. Shredded cabbage is occasionally added, though I find this is often used as a filler when the other ingredients are scarce. Finally, the salad is dressed with groundnut or sesame oil and a generous squeeze of lime. *Lahpet thoke* is made at home as snack or ordered in teashops, cafes and restaurants as a specific dish (whereas *a-hlu lahpet* will be presented at the end of a meal as standard).

The funny thing is that when I was a kid, one of my cousins and I used to love eating *lahpet* mixed with plain rice, which really wasn't the done thing. We particularly enjoyed eating it out of an enamel bowl with a spoon. The rest of our family used to mock us mercilessly for being weird and gauche, but now 25 years later, *lahpet htamin* ('pickled tea rice') can be seen on the menus of all the hippest joints in town.

As delicious as *lahpet* is, it's also adored for its ability to keep you pepped up. Compared to other forms of tea, it has the maximum rate of caffeine, so students studying for exams and those attending the all-night musical theatre shows (known as *pwè*) will fill up on the stuff. In fact, pregnant women in Burma and anyone with a heart condition are strongly advised to avoid *lahpet*, and it was one of the things I missed the most when I was expecting myself. Moreover, one of the reasons that *lahpet* is served after a meal is because it's thought to act as a kind of digestif.

Talking of digestifs, I'll leave you with this little anecdote. For much of my childhood, I was genuinely concerned that if I ever dared to nap after eating, I would suddenly be transformed into a horrible snake, because that's what my parents warned me, and the stories I read in my favourite comic *Shwe Thway* only served to back them up. It was only when I was much older (probably too old) that I understood that this was a hoary legend told to Burmese children in order to prevent them getting indigestion. To be honest, I'm not sure I'll ever completely forgive them.

Staple Ingredients & Suitable Alternatives

These are the staples that you'll find in any Burmese kitchen. I've listed alternatives where you might not be able to find the real thing.

Fresh ingredients

Coriander (cilantro)
The default garnish in so many Burmese curries, noodles and salads that it's almost a joke, but we're keen on using more than the leaves. The stems are an essential part of various curry bases, pounded together with other ingredients to give a green, earthy note. Try to find coriander that's almost bolted/has feathery leaves as this will give the most pungent flavour and is most similar to Burmese coriander (after all, we call it *nan nan bin* – 'smelly smelly plant'!).

Fresh chillies
Fresh green finger chillies are ground up as the base for the hotter dishes and are also used whole in others. Bird's eye chillies are also occasionally used according to the cook's preference e.g. in salads.

Garlic
Most dishes start with a base of fried onions and garlic. Garlic also crops up in countless dishes: in the salad dressing, infused in oil, in salsa and as a fried garnish (Crispy Fried Garlic, page 238). Some types of Burmese garlic are so sweet and mild that their cloves are even eaten raw as a snack – raw cloves are also eaten with Shan Sour Rice (page 102) and Mandalay Chicken Noodle Salad (page 117). Garlic powder is also used in batters.

Ginger
Many dishes have fresh ginger as one of the base ingredients, although ground ginger is popular, too. Ginger is also eaten in its pickled form in dips, Pickled Tea Salad (page 63) and Pickled Ginger and Sesame Salad (page 79).

Limes
Lime juice is used in most salad dressings, dips and condiments. Lime wedges are used to squeeze over noodle dishes.

Ngapi
Iconic in Burma as an ingredient that provides umami as well as saltiness. Literally meaning 'pressed fish', but made from fermented fish or small fry and occasionally shrimp, and mixed with salt (see also The Food of Burma, page 25). Shrimp paste is a good substitute (see also page 260). Various forms of *ngapi* are turned into curries, dips and side dishes. For most recipes in this book calling for shrimp paste, the wet stuff sold in jars (available from most supermarkets) is fine, but try to track down the type in blocks available at Asian supermarkets to make *balachaung* on page 211.

Onions
Most dishes start with a base of fried onions and garlic. It is also an ingredient that appears raw in many salads and is even eaten raw in wedges with Burmese Fried Chicken (page 148) or Burmese Chicken Nuggets (page 156) in the same way you might eat pickled onions with a pork pie. Crispy Fried Onions (page 238) are an essential garnish in Burmese cuisine, as is the onion oil that is the result of making said crispy onions.

Spring onions (scallions)
These are used as an adjunct to onions in bases as they give a sweeter and fresher allium note. They are also shredded and used as a garnish for noodles and curries.

Tamarind
Used in many dips and condiments as well as curries to provide a sweet and sour note. It's best to make your own tamarind juice, but tamarind paste and the concentrate is fine – just remember that tamarind paste is often sweetened so adjust the seasoning accordingly as needed.

Tomatoes
Ripe tomatoes are a common ingredient in many curry bases. Green tomatoes tend to be used in salads.

Store-cupboard ingredients

Dried chilli
Dried chilli flakes for making roasted chilli flakes or Chilli Oil (page 236), chilli powder as an ingredient and dried whole chillies.

Dried shrimp
Tiny dried prawns sold in packets in Asian supermarkets, used whole or blended to a floss or powder.

Fish sauce (*nam pla*)
Burmese cooks tend to use fish sauce where the rest of Asia uses soy sauce. Liquid aminos makes a good vegetarian substitute (Marigold or Braggs). You can even get vegetarian fish sauce now made from seaweed (Thai Taste or Longdan).

Flours
Rice flour and glutinous rice flour are primarily used in Burmese cooking. Essential for making batters and doughs, these flours are also used as thickeners. Where used as a thickener, cornstarch can be substituted.

Groundnut oil (peanut oil)
Used for shallow and deep-frying and also in salad and noodle dressings. Any neutral-tasting oil such as rapeseed or sunflower oil is an acceptable substitute.

MSG
A granulated seasoning, full name monosodium glutamate, that enhances the savouriness of a dish (that fifth taste known as *umami*) in the same way that sugar makes dishes sweeter or salt makes dishes saltier. Known in Burmese as *a-cho hmont* meaning 'sweet powder', our favourite brand is the original Japanese AJI-NO-MOTO, and we like to add a pinch to most savoury dishes. (See page 37 for more.)

Paprika
None of that smoked or hot stuff for us – in all our curries, we use plain paprika which we call it *a-yaun din hmont* or 'colour-enhancing powder'.

Rice
Burmese rice is halfway in taste and texture between jasmine and basmati, so I like to use a mix of the two.

Salt
Coarse sea salt is fine. Most saltiness is provided by fish sauce and *ngapi*.

Turmeric
Ground turmeric is more common than fresh and is used in many traditional Burmese dishes – as a marinade for fish or chicken, as a base for many curries and in chutneys and pickles – to add colour, fragrance and a bittersweet note. Turmeric is also popular for its medicinal and antibacterial qualities and apparently good for asthma.

A typical kitchen at a Burmese htamin zain *which literally means 'rice shop', i.e. a restaurant serving traditional rice and curries. Note the charcoal braziers, the two-handled wok on the wall and the handle-less saucepans.*

Dried chilli 'pick and mix' at a City Mart supermarket in Yangon.

Why MSG is A-OKAY

For decades, monosodium glutamate has been unfairly maligned as being some kind of nasty chemical that causes all sorts of side effects (historically known as 'Chinese restaurant syndrome'). Whilst there's no denying that some people have experienced unfortunate symptoms after having ingested MSG, there has never been any scientific evidence that MSG itself is the cause of any of them, and so, although these reactions may be real, it is likely they are a result of a negative placebo effect (known as 'nocebo effect').

MSG is present in a plethora of popular processed foods, including KFC, Quavers, gravy granules and instant soups (look for 'flavour enhancer E621', 'hydrolysed protein' and 'autolyzed yeast' as well as MSG on packaging labels). It's also known as Ve-Tsin or gourmet powder, and is the main component of Aromat, Maggi seasoning, Accent, Knorr chicken powder, Knorr pork granules, Zest, Začin C and countless other instant stocks and seasonings embraced around the world – if it was really as demonic as it's made out to be, it would have been banned long ago. Noted chefs such as David Chang and Heston Blumenthal have spoken out in vigorous defence of the stuff, and celebrated chef and writer Anthony Bourdain straight out said, 'You know what causes Chinese restaurant syndrome? Racism.'

Sometimes I wonder if a rebrand is necessary. No one would want to use salt if it was sold as 'sodium chloride', so maybe MSG should be sold as 'flavour crystals' or 'umami pearls'* or something else equally appealing.

For more information on the history of, and the science behind, MSG please do read Tim Anderson's piece 'The War on MSG', Helen Rosner's 'An MSG Convert Visits the High Church of Umami', John Mahoney's 'The Notorious MSG's Unlikely Formula for Success', and Anna Maria Barry-Jester 'How MSG Got a Bad Rap: Flawed Science and Xenophobia'.

However, if you still have qualms about using MSG even after reading all that, I'll try my best not to judge you, and you can always use a glug of Japanese dashi, a pinch of Marigold bouillon or a chunk of a Kallo stock cube instead. It's really not a deal-breaker. But as for me, I'll continue to use MSG happily, because the Burmese, we're pretty damned fond of the stuff.

* The latter name suggested to me by food writer Sejal Sukhadwala.

Spiders i.e. skimmers used for removing food from hot oil or boiling water (called a 'spider' because the basket looks like a web).

More tools for sale. From left to right: spade heads, kitchen scissors, charcoal tongs and mont lin mayar pans.

Equipment in the Burmese Kitchen

The traditional Burmese kitchen would be found in a separate outhouse, like at my grandparents' house in Mandalay. This was to prevent smoke and fumes from getting into the house and to stop fire from spreading, as cooking was always done over an open flame (my mum remembers having to bury the cinders every night). We don't have a tradition of ovens in Burma – our only cake is more of a pudding and is cooked on a stovetop. My eldest aunt actually had two kitchens at her house in Yangon – a modern Western-style one within the house with an electric cooker that was very rarely used except when my uncle had a notion to grill some meat ('Barbecue time!' he'd announce), and an outhouse kitchen next to their garage, which is where all the cooking was actually done.

In Burma, power cuts frequently occur and electricity is expensive, so not only have we not tended to use cookers, we've never relied on fridges either, and ingredients are still bought fresh from the market bright and early each day.

Even now, you will probably see the following equipment in a Burmese kitchen (more or less in order of size as well as importance):

Kitchen table
Small, low, round wooden table similar to our traditional dining table. Most food is leisurely prepared at this table whilst sitting cross-legged on the floor or with your legs folded to one side – it can also be stored upright out of the way when not in use. Also good for playing cards!

Meat safe
Known as a 'cat-safe' in Burma, this is a raised wooden cupboard with wire mesh doors where raw meat and fish for the day was kept. Now generally used for cooked food, although my grandma stored hand-rolled turmeric and honey pills and other homemade herbal concoctions in hers.

Stove
Originally, this would have been a wood-fire pit, but latterly an earthenware wood-burning or charcoal brazier or a metal kerosene stove. Electric cookers are becoming more common now though, especially in urban areas.

Rice cooker
Our main concession to modernity. Practically everyone in Asia uses a rice cooker now and they're a godsend. You just set it and forget about it, and you get perfect rice every time.

You don't need a fancy Japanese neuro-fuzzy one that costs a lot – a cheap one from Argos will do.

Aluminium cooking pots
Known in Burmese as *dan-oh* ('aluminium pot') and known in English by its Indian name *degchi*, these are our universal cooking pots. They have lids, but no handles and they stack neatly inside each other when not in use. Standard saucepans (even non-stick) are fine to use instead.

Earthenware cooking pots
Known in Burmese as *myay-oh* ('earth pot'), these pre-date the aluminium pots and are still used for slow-cooking and braising. Slow cookers and casseroles are fine to use instead.

Frying pans
Used when shallow-frying such as for Crispy Fried Garlic (page 238) or Crispy Fried Onions (page 238) or when dry-frying such as for Toasted Gram Flour (page 240). Standard frying pans (even non-stick) are fine to use instead.

Woks with two ring handles are used for deep-frying. Standard Chinese woks are fine to use instead.

Kettle
Traditional Burmese kettles are huge metal affairs that are heated straight on the fire. Electric kettles are of course fine to use instead.

Oil pot
A metal pot with a lid for storing 'Cooked' Oil or oil leftover from frying for re-use i.e. *si chet*. You can buy oil pots online – look for 'grease keeper' (horrific name, I know).

Winnowing tray
Made from bamboo, these round trays are used for cleaning rice, dried beans and vegetables. A tea tray would suffice.

Colander
These are essential for draining and rinsing noodles after they have been cooked, but also for resting fritters after they have been fried so that any residual grease drains away.

Pestle and mortar
Often I have woken up to the sound of ingredients being pounded for the day – garlic, ginger, chillies, dried shrimp.

Although it's easy to use a mini-chopper or blender instead, it's often quite therapeutic to bash away. Burmese pestle and mortars are made from rough granite, which really helps with grinding, especially when salt is added as is often the case.

Cleaver
Necessary for jointing chicken, and chopping and mincing meat.

Chopper
Resembles a cleaver, but with a thinner blade and used to slice, chop and shred vegetables and herbs.

Cook's knife
Used for peeling fruit and vegetables. The Burmese always peel away from themselves.

Spider
A type of skimmer in the form of a shallow wire-mesh basket with a long handle, used for removing food from hot oil (called a 'spider' because the basket looks like a web). I actually prefer to use an *ami jakushi* – the finer meshed Japanese version – as it's easier to remove rogue pieces of batter from the wok or pan when making fritters. Slotted spoons and scoop colanders such as the one made by Joseph Joseph are also good.

Chopsticks
Used for stirring or tossing ingredients when frying or cooking, and also for extracting individual items from liquid or hot oil. Feel free to use slotted spoons or tongs instead.

My grandparents' cook Aunty Thay and my father's nanny Pwa Ahnt (who lived with my grandparents until she died) preparing food together in the outhouse kitchen at home in Mandalay.

Cover Versions

As a child, my musical tastes were largely dictated by my parents. Having arrived in the UK just before I was born, their choices largely consisted of the 'safe' Western music that had been permitted to infiltrate Burma – for example: ABBA, Andy Williams and a certain Cliff Richard – as well as old-time Burmese songs, some of which dated from before World War II as far as I could tell.

Later on, however, as we kept in touch with the family back home, our playlists began to be dominated by the music of a man called Zaw Win Htut.

I say 'a man' – he was (and, to be honest, still is) lauded as a rock legend in Burma – a Burmese Bruce Springsteen at the very height of his powers. I adored every single one of his songs – the power ballads and the roaring anthems – and I would lustily yell along to the mixtapes we brought back from every visit to the old country.

One fine day here in England though, I remember very clearly that my family were all in the car on the way to visit my greataunt and greatuncle in Surrey, and for once we had the radio on, rather than one of my parents' cassettes, when suddenly the mellow voice of John Lennon filled the air (although I didn't recognise who it was at the time).

I stopped bickering with my elder brothers as confusion clouded my features, and then I unwrinkled my brow and suddenly yelped, 'Hey, this is a cover of one of Zaw Win Htut's songs? I never realised he was so famous'.

Of course, I was wrong. So very wrong. In fact, this was just the first time I'd heard the original version of 'The Ballad of John and Yoko'. Zaw Win Htut's song was the cover, not the Beatles'.

My youthful world came tumbling down. 'Cocaine' was actually an Eric Clapton number. 'The First Cut is the Deepest', a Rod Stewart track.

And a few years later, I had another rude awakening when I finally twigged that one of my favourite dishes *kyet-thar gon baun-gyi kyaw* was actually a culinary cover version of the Sichuan dish *gong bao* chicken (or '*kung pao*' as the West would have it).

But you know what? I still prefer the covers by Zaw Win Htut, and I'd still rather have the Burmese riffs on those dishes. Neither may be as edgy as the originals, but there's a sweetness to both that is irresistible.*

This is a very roundabout segue into me telling you two things, gentle reader.

Firstly, there are several recipes in this collection that will make you go, 'Hang on a minute, that reminds me of an Indian dish' or 'Wait a second, I'm sure I had something like that in our local Chinese.' And my response to you is, you're probably right, but where I am aware or even suspect that this might be the case, I have mentioned it in the introduction to that recipe.

Secondly, the Burmese love adapting dishes from other cuisines so very much that had I kept to my original table of contents, you'd be looking at a cookbook at least twice the length. But for my own sanity (and that of my publisher's), I whittled the list down by excluding anything that was too close to the original, rather than an affectionate tribute on our part. So, despite the Burmese love for eating *aloo poori*, *samosas* and *paratha*, there are no recipes for them here. Neither will you find the recipe for our version of *gong bao* chicken that I mentioned above, but fret not – that one's actually already on my blog at www.meemalee.com – and that's where I'll continue to put the rest of our culinary covers, so I hope this will appease you and please do stay tuned…

* As an interesting side note, Zaw Win Htut's Wikipedia entry states 'Like most Burmese pop singers, Zaw Win Htut became famous with Burmese language covers of foreign (mostly Western rock and pop) hits' but, unlike most, he 'was actually embarrassed about it', saying that singing those songs was 'like wearing someone else's shirt'. Zaw Win Htut now makes original music, and bloody good it is too.

Fritters

A-KYAW-ZONE

Fritters of various kinds are a favourite breakfast item in Burma, as well as a welcome treat with a meal or a snack with a punchy dip. In short, the Burmese love to eat fried stuff at any time of day, especially served hot from the wok. Burmese fritters work particularly well as a garnish for starchy food, especially sticky rice and noodles. Unlike a lot of our other foods, they also tend to be vegan or at least vegetarian.

Burmese Tofu Fritters

TOHU KYAW   တိုဟူးကြော်

As a child, I never understood why tofu was a dirty word until I discovered that 'tofu' in Burma is unlike any other. The soybean stuff which, rather than tofu, we call *pe pyar* (literally 'bean slab') is more of a blank canvas and often woefully misused, but in Burma, we use chickpeas or split peas for a tofu that is both delicious in itself and also so much easier to make. The original Shan tofu is made from split peas and is a creamy yellow, but the Burmese version is made from chickpeas and is more golden. Our tofu is versatile enough to be used as a topping for noodles in its molten form before it's even set, in salads in its set form and as this moreish fritter.

There's no shame in using shortcuts by the way – though for Shan tofu, fresh or dried pulses would be ground from scratch, the Burmese version is more often made from gram flour – and both versions are vegan and gluten-free to boot! Make a batch of these fritters as a starter or as canapés or even as a beer snack, and watch as people burn their tongues in their haste to eat as many as possible.

Serves 4-6

groundnut oil or other
   neutral-tasting oil, for
   greasing and frying
100g gram flour
¼ teaspoon salt
¼ teaspoon MSG or ½
   tablespoon chicken or
   vegetable bouillon
¼ teaspoon ground turmeric
¼ teaspoon baking powder
Tamarind Dipping Sauce
   (page 237), to serve

Grease a 15 x 20cm rectangular container with oil and set to one side.

Place the flour, salt, MSG, turmeric and baking powder and 350ml of water into a large bowl and whisk thoroughly. Cover and leave somewhere cool for 2 hours, whisking once every half an hour.

Add 250ml of just-boiled water and 2 tablespoons of oil to a large saucepan and set over a high heat. Bring to a vigorous boil, pour in the flour-turmeric mixture and begin stirring with a large wooden spoon. Reduce the heat to medium-high. Continue stirring for 3–5 minutes, or until the mixture is fragrant and bubbling – the consistency should become a thick, silky soup. This is now *tohu nway*, molten tofu (literally 'tofu warm'), which should be used immediately as a topping for *tohu nway* noodles (see Cook's Note).

Continue stirring the tofu mixture for a further 3–5 minutes, or until craters form on the surface and it is the consistency of very thick custard. Pour into the greased container and leave at room temperature for 1 hour, or until set.

Drain away any liquid that comes out and then wrap the tofu in kitchen paper and return to the container. At this point, you can cover the container with clingfilm or a lid and refrigerate until needed. It will keep for 48 hours and can now also be used for Burmese tofu salad (page 72).

…continued on page 46

When you're ready to fry the fritters, unwrap the tofu and slice it into roughly 3cm-sided triangles of 1cm thickness. Try to avoid making any cracks or jagged edges as these will cause the fritters to collapse in the hot oil.

Heat a 5cm depth of oil in a wok or large saucepan over a high heat until you can feel waves of heat come off with the palm of your hand. Using a tablespoon, gently drop the triangles into the hot oil, until the surface of the wok is covered, but make sure the triangles do not touch. Let the fritters fry for 2–4 minutes, until you can see them crisp up and turn golden around the edges, and then flip them gently and fry for another 2–4 minutes. Remove with a slotted spoon and place in a colander set over a dish or frying pan to drain. Continue with the remaining fritters, frying in batches to avoid crowding.

Now fry the fritters again in larger batches; this time you can add more fritters to the wok as the initial frying means they will not stick together. Fry for 2–3 minutes, until they are crisp. Remove and drain the fritters on plenty of kitchen paper, and serve immediately with tamarind dipping sauce (page 237).

Cook's Note

This recipe is actually for a variant known as *na-pyan kyaw* ('twice fried') from the town of Taunggyi in the Shan State. It makes for a much crisper fritter, yet still meltingly soft inside.

Standard *tohu kyaw* is made as follows: slice the tofu into rectangles of 5cm x 3cm and 1cm thickness and then make two parallel slashes all the way through the centre of each rectangle. Fry as above (but only fry once) and serve immediately as a garnish for Shan Noodles (page 114), or as a snack with the dipping sauce, before the fritters lose their crispness.

Tohu nway noodles are a variant of Shan Noodles – simply pour the molten tofu on top and garnish with pea shoots.

A variety of dried fish from Burma. Fried in a little oil, dried fish is probably the most basic and favourite of Burmese snacks.

Bottle Gourd Fritters

BUTHI KYAW ဘူးသီးကြော်

These fritters are considered the quintessential Burmese *a-kyaw*, usually
making an appearance whenever friends and family gather, but they can
be hard to get right and too often the batter will flake off leaving the poor,
naked gourd inside, looking like a dismal version of tempura. The trick is to
make sure that each piece is encased in batter, which should be thick enough
that when you hold the fritters upright it doesn't drip off. Your reward is a
crunchy golden shell rather like that of a nice piece of cod from your local
fish and chip shop.

Serves 6-8

400g bottle gourd (*dudhi*)
  or chayote
groundnut oil or other neutral-
  tasting oil, for frying
Tamarind Dipping Sauce
  (page 237), to serve

For the batter
6 tablespoons rice flour
4 tablespoons glutinous rice flour
2 tablespoons self-raising flour
1 teaspoon baking powder
1 teaspoon garlic powder
1 teaspoon ground ginger
⅓ over-ripe mashed banana
  (about 30g)
salt and freshly ground
  black pepper

Combine the batter ingredients in a bowl and add 130ml of water to form
the consistency of wallpaper paste.

Peel the bottle gourd and then slice into 1cm x 1cm x 8cm sticks. Add the
gourd to the batter and then toss, making sure each piece is thickly covered
in the batter.

Heat a 6cm depth of oil in a wok or large frying pan over a medium-high heat
(or use a deep-fat fryer). When you can feel waves of heat coming off the oil,
carefully and slowly lower 2–3 pieces of gourd into the hot oil – disperse them
a little to make sure they don't stick together.

Fry the gourd pieces for 3–4 minutes, until the edges of each fritter start
to brown. Flip them gently and fry for another 3–4 minutes. They should be
golden brown by now with a crisp batter shell.

Remove the fritters from the oil with a slotted spoon and drain on plenty of
kitchen paper. Repeat until all the fritters have been made, and then serve
immediately with tamarind dipping sauce (page 237).

Split Pea Crackers

PE KYAW/PE GYAN KYAW ပဲကြော် / ပဲခြမ်းကြော်

A traditional accompaniment to *mohinga* (Fish Noodle Soup, page 107), our national dish, and sometimes Coconut Chicken Noodles (page 109), these crackers can be made from whatever pulses you have handy (in which case you'd call them *pe kyaw*) though split peas are most common (and these ones are called *pe gyan kyaw*). They're delicate and crispy, just like the ones made by my favourite *mohinga* cycle vendor in Mandalay who cooks them fresh every morning. Eat them as a snack, on the side or broken over said noodle soups or even use them like croutons.

Makes 6 large crackers

75g yellow split peas or toor dal
¼ teaspoon bicarbonate of soda
2 tablespoons rice flour
2 tablespoons self-raising flour
1 tablespoon glutinous rice flour
¼ teaspoon salt
¼ teaspoon MSG or ½
    tablespoon chicken or
    vegetable bouillon
pinch of ground turmeric
groundnut oil or other neutral-
    tasting oil, for frying

Add the peas and the bicarbonate of soda to a mixing bowl with plenty of water and soak overnight.

The next day, drain the peas thoroughly and return to the bowl along with 100ml of fresh water, the flours, salt, MSG and turmeric. Whisk well to form a runny batter and set aside for at least 30 minutes.

Fill a 28cm frying pan halfway with oil and heat over a medium-high until you can feel waves of heat come off with the palm of your hand.

Whisk the batter again as the peas will have settled at the bottom of the bowl. Scoop out half a ladleful of batter, making sure you have some peas in the mix. Pour carefully into the hot oil. It will spread and puff into a lacy cracker. Do this again until the surface of the pan is covered, but make sure the fritters do not touch. You should be able to make two or three crackers at a time. The edges of each cracker may break away and escape – use a spatula to scoop these edges gently back over the cracker – it's fine if they overlap slightly.

Fry for 2–4 minutes, or until golden round the edges, and then flip them gently and fry for another 2–4 minutes. Remove the crackers with a slotted spoon and drain on plenty of kitchen paper – they will crisp up. Serve with *mohinga* (page 107), Burmese coconut chicken noodles (page 109) or with any of the dipping sauces (pages 236–237).

Mandalay Bean Fritters

MANDALAY PE KYAW

These kidney bean fritters are ridiculously easy to make and dangerously quick to disappear. Like the majority of our fried snacks, they're vegan, but unlike most, these are just as good reheated in a dry frying pan or in the oven. They should be soft and fluffy inside and have the thinnest, crispest shell outside. Eat these bean fritters with any of the dipping sauces.

Makes 10-15 fritters

400g tin red kidney beans
1 red onion, diced
1 tablespoon self-raising flour
1 tablespoon rice flour
1 tablespoon glutinous rice flour
1 teaspoon baking powder
1 teaspoon ground ginger
1 teaspoon garlic powder
½ teaspoon salt
¼ teaspoon MSG or ½
  tablespoon chicken or
  vegetable bouillon
groundnut oil or other neutral-
  tasting oil, for frying
Tamarind Dipping Sauce
  (page 237), to serve

Drain most of the liquid from the tin of beans and then empty the beans and the residual sludge into a large bowl. Mash the beans with a fork till they are broken up.

Add the onion and the dry ingredients to the bowl and mix well.

Heat a 5cm depth of oil in a large saucepan or wok over a medium-high heat until you can feel waves of heat come off with the palm of your hand.

Using a tablespoon, scoop one spoonful after another of the bean mixture into the hot oil, until the surface of the pan is covered, but make sure the fritters do not touch. Let them fry for 2–4 minutes, until you can see them brown round the edges and then flip gently and fry for another 2–4 minutes. Remove the fritters with a slotted spoon and drain on plenty of kitchen paper. Serve with tamarind dipping sauce (page 237).

Cook's Note
Unlike most fritters these can be reheated easily in a dry frying pan, or in a moderate oven (180°C/160°C Fan/Gas Mark 4).

Mandalay Black Gram Fritters

MANDALAY BAYA KYAW　မန္တလေးဘယာကြော်

There are two types of *baya kyaw* in Burma, the Burmese cousin to the Indian *vada* fritters (for the other type see Yangon Chickpea Fritters, page 57). If you ask for *baya kyaw* in Mandalay, you will get these fritters made from split black gram (or urad dal) – crunchy on the outside and soft on the inside, and similar to Indian *medu vada*. It's also known as *Bamar baya kyaw* (Burman vada) and in Yangon and Mogok as *matpe kyaw*, 'matpe' bean being another name for the pulse that's used.

Mandalay *baya kyaw* is often eaten as a salad (follow the recipe for Shredded Chicken and Tomato Salad, page 71, but swap these for the chicken and tomato). It's also snipped as a garnish over *mohinga* (page 107) or Mandalay Chicken Noodle Salad (page 117), or served as a snack or on the side with any dipping sauce.

Makes 15 doughnuts
or 30 small fritters

groundnut or other neutral-tasting oil, for deep-frying
Tamarind Dipping Sauce (page 237), to serve

For the fritters
200g urad dal (split black gram)
2 medium onions, roughly chopped
2 garlic cloves, peeled
5cm piece of banana, peeled
2 tablespoons self-raising flour
2 teaspoons bicarbonate of soda
1 teaspoon sugar
1 teaspoon salt
¼ teaspoon MSG or ½ tablespoon chicken or vegetable bouillon

Soak the dal in a large bowl of water overnight. Drain and add to a blender or food processor along with the remaining fritter ingredients. Blitz to a rough paste, then decant back into the bowl and stir. Leave the dal mixture to rest, uncovered, in the fridge for 1 hour, then remove and stir. The mixture should be firm enough for a spoon to stand upright in it.

Heat a 6cm depth of oil in a wok or large saucepan over a high heat (or use a deep-fat fryer).

To make the doughnuts, wet your hands and then scoop a golf ball of the dal mixture into one moistened palm and then flatten into a 6cm diameter patty. Poke a hole in the middle with the moistened index finger of your other hand and then, very carefully, slide the patty gently off your palm into the hot oil, taking care to avoid burning yourself.

Repeat until the pan is full, but avoid crowding the pan otherwise the patties will stick (3–4 patties should fit, depending on pan size).

To make the small fritters, use a tablespoon to drop ping-pong-sized balls into the hot oil until the pan is full, again leaving enough room to make sure they don't stick together (5–7 balls should fit, depending on your pan size).

Turn the heat down to medium-high and wait 3–4 minutes until the edges of each fritter brown and then flip them gently and leave for another 3–4 minutes, until golden brown all over. Remove from the oil with a slotted spoon and drain on plenty of kitchen paper. Make more *baya kyaw* until all the mixture has been used, and then serve immediately with tamarind dipping sauce (page 237).

Yangon Chickpea Fritters

YANGON BAYA KYAW   ရန်ကုန်ဘယာကြော်

If you ask for *baya kyaw* in Yangon, you will get a crunchier fritter made from
yellow split peas or this variation that I prefer made from chickpeas studded
with roasted chana dal (daria dal).

These *baya kyaw* are a little more like pakora with their Indian spicing and
should be made as small morsels that you can just pop in your mouth.

Makes 20 fritters

400g tin chickpeas, drained
1 medium onion, halved
1 green finger chilli
6 fresh or dried curry leaves
handful of coriander leaves
100g daria dal (roasted chana
   dal) or roasted peas
3 tablespoons gram flour
1 teaspoon ground cumin
1 teaspoon salt
groundnut oil or other neutral-
   tasting oil, for frying

Add the drained chickpeas, one of the onion halves, the chilli, curry leaves
and coriander to a blender or food processor and blitz to a rough paste.

Finely chop the other onion half and place in a mixing bowl. Add the dal,
flour, cumin and salt, and mix. Scoop the chickpea paste into the bowl and
mix again.

Heat a 5cm depth of oil in a wok or large saucepan until you can feel waves
of heat come off with the palm of your hand. Using a tablespoon, scoop one
spoonful after another of the chickpea mixture into the hot oil, until the surface
of the wok is covered, making sure the fritters do not touch. Let them fry for
2–4 minutes until you can see them brown around the edges and then flip them
gently and fry for another 2–4 minutes. Remove the fritters with a slotted spoon
and drain on plenty of kitchen paper. Serve with any of the dipping sauces on
pages 236–237.

Cook's Note
Unlike most fritters, these can be reheated easily in a dry frying pan or in
the oven.

'Husband & Wife' Snacks

MONT LIN MAYAR   မုန့်လင်မယား

These are little crispy rounded pancakes filled with whole yellow peas or chickpeas, spring onions and sometimes fresh tomato, which are fried and then stuck together to make a harmonious whole – hence the name, which literally means 'husband and wife snacks'. Similar to Vietnamese *banh khot* pancakes, they're made in huge, beautiful pans that remind me of steel drums. When I was little, it became fashionable in Burma for the vendors to fill the pancakes with quail eggs instead of the traditional peas, although this type is usually sold as separate halves rather than combined, contrary to the coupled-up name. I have to say I probably prefer the more modern version as it's quite fun biting into the tiny yolks.

Makes 24 halves
or 12 whole snacks

For the batter
2cm piece of ginger
100g rice flour
1 teaspoon salt
½ teaspoon sugar
½ teaspoon bicarbonate of soda
¼ teaspoon MSG or ½
   tablespoon chicken or
   vegetable bouillon

For the filling
2 tablespoons tinned chickpeas
   or pigeon peas
2 spring onions, green parts
   only, shredded
12 quail eggs

You will need to have one of the
   following tins (see recipe introduction)
banh khot
khanom krok
takoyaki
aebleskiver
poffertjes
mini muffin
tartlet

Pound the ginger to a pulp using a mortar and pestle (or use a food processor and blitz). Pour any ginger juice that comes out into a mixing bowl and then use your hands to squeeze the ginger pulp to get the rest of the ginger juice. Discard the ginger pulp.

Add the rest of the batter ingredients and 250ml of water to the bowl. Whisk briskly, cover and leave to rest for 2 hours.

Generously grease the tin that you are using and then heat in the oven preheated to its highest temperature or place the pan directly on the stovetop over a high heat (whichever option is appropriate for your pan).

Pour the batter into each hole in the prepared pan to come just over halfway. Allow the pancakes to cook for 5 minutes until they start to sear and crisp on the bottom (after a minute or two, the batter will rise up the sides of each hole to form little pancakes). Add a few peas and spring onions to half of the pancakes and crack quail eggs into rest.

If cooking in the oven, wait a minute or two until the egg whites turn opaque before serving. If cooking on the stovetop, cover with a lid and cook until the egg whites turn opaque before serving. Remove and keep warm while making another batch until the batter has been used up.

Serve immediately as a snack by themselves or with any of the dipping sauces on pages 236–237.

Salads

A-THOKE-SONE

အသုပ်စုံ

A salad is not just a salad in Burma. Forget limp lettuce leaves with a drizzle of oil – like salads in Thailand and Laos, a Burmese salad can be hot or cold, leafy or chunky, mild or spicy, a dainty side dish or a whacking great meal of its own.

The name *a-thoke* comes from the action you use when making the salad – I usually say it means 'tossed' but, to be honest, this is a pale translation, as the same verb is used when referring to someone painting a surface or wiping something away. Perhaps the Karate Kid doing his 'wax on, wax off' routine conveys the grace of the phrase best.

What makes our salads even more exciting is that they often use ingredients beyond your wildest dreams – favourites include fresh lemons, pickled ginger and, best of all, Burma's legendary pickled tea leaves, *lahpet*.

Pickled Tea Leaf Salad

LAHPET THOKE   လက်ဖက်သုပ်

Lahpet or pickled tea is the most iconic of Burmese foods and unique to
the country. It's eaten in two main ways – *a-hlu lahpet* (pictured) also known
as *Mandalay lahpet*, and *lahpet thoke* also known as *Yangon lahpet*. To learn
more about *lahpet* and its huge significance in Burma, please do read the
section on Eating & Serving Customs, pages 30–33.

    Lahpet thoke is excellent as a snack, eaten with plain rice, or at the end of
a meal, but I wouldn't recommend serving it with other dishes, as it deserves
to take centre stage. You can buy *lahpet* online from Bayin Foods, or Mum's
House (see Stockists, page 262), but at a pinch, you can substitute preserved
artichokes, as they're bittersweet, savoury and astringent in a similar way.

Serves 2

20g *lahpet* or 6 preserved
    artichoke hearts, finely
    chopped
handful of dried shrimp
2 white cabbage leaves,
    shredded
1 medium tomato, sliced
sprinkle of sesame seeds
handful of Crispy Fried Garlic
    (page 238) or shop-bought
    fried garlic
handful of fried broad beans or
    roasted chana dal (daria dal)
handful of Fried Red-skin
    Peanuts (page 240) or
    salted peanuts
1 tablespoon groundnut oil or
    other neutral-tasting oil
juice of ¼ lime
1 finger chilli, sliced (optional)

Mix all the ingredients in a bowl. Eat as a snack at the end of a meal or with rice.

Citrus & Shallot Salad

SHAUK THI THOKE   ရှောက်သီးသုပ်

The name of this dish just means 'lemon salad' – we Burmese are known for being laconic. I realise that a lemon salad doesn't sound like something you should be attempting, unless you want to make your face scrunch up in pain like those YouTube videos of poor unsuspecting babies, but trust me – it's wonderful. It does start with a wallop of sour and spice, but then mellows out into savoury goodness and you'll come back for more.

When I was little and heard that an older cousin was engaged to an Englishman, we had the usual fear of, 'but will he like our food?' but the first time I met him, he was merrily tucking into a dish of this, and we all laughed and breathed a sigh of relief! Although you can eat it by itself like he did, it's a lovely accompaniment for rich curries as it provides a sharp contrast. It also goes particularly well with the Wood Ear and Glass Noodle Soup (page 113) and they're often served together.

Serves 4

3 lemons
2 tablespoons fish sauce
1 medium onion or 2 banana
 shallots
1 tablespoon dried shrimp
1 teaspoon shrimp paste
1 tablespoon Toasted Gram Flour
 (page 240)
1 tablespoon groundnut oil
1 teaspoon chilli flakes
1 green finger chilli, sliced
 into rings

Peel the lemons as you would peel an orange and then slice them crosswise into thin rounds so they resemble Murakami flowers (roughly torn segments are more traditional, but this method is so beautiful, I can never resist).

Place the lemon slices in a bowl and drizzle the fish sauce all over. Leave the lemon to marinate for 10 minutes.

Peel the onion or shallots and slice crosswise into rings as thinly as possible. Place in a small bowl with cold water and leave to soak until ready to use.

Blitz the dried shrimp in a blender or pound using a mortar and pestle until you have a texture resembling dust.

In another small bowl, mix the shrimp paste, shrimp dust, gram flour and oil. Pour in the fish sauce from the marinated lemons and mix again to make the dressing.

Drain the onion rings thoroughly. Get a serving dish and place a layer of onion in the bottom followed by a layer of lemon. Drizzle half of the dressing over the lemon and then add another layer of onion and layer of lemon. Drizzle the rest of the dressing all over.

Scatter the chilli flakes and green chilli over the salad and serve as a side dish to wood ear and glass noodle soup (page 113) or with braised beef curry (page 134).

Green Bean Salad

PE THI THOKE   ပဲသီးသုပ်

This is a very simple dish that's eaten as an accompaniment to other heartier fare. A variation of the dish, called *pe thi pein*, is made by boiling the green beans until completely wilted (rather than just blanching) and then adding a teaspoon of tamarind paste to the tomato sauce before continuing with the rest of the recipe.

Serves 4

2 tablespoons groundnut oil
  or other neutral-tasting oil
200g tinned plum tomatoes,
  diced
1 medium onion, diced
250g green beans
1 tablespoon smooth or crunchy
  peanut butter
1 tablespoon fish sauce
juice of ½ lime

Heat the oil in a saucepan over a medium heat, add the tomatoes and onion, and simmer for 1 hour. Set to one side to cool.

Trim the beans and then chop them in half. Place in a bowl and pour over boiling water to scald them. Drain and then stir the cooled tomato sauce through the beans. Add the peanut butter, fish sauce and lime juice, and mix thoroughly. Serve.

Cook's Note
Traditionally, salted peanuts are ground to a paste with a little water and added to this dish, but life is short so I use peanut butter.

Egg & Lettuce Salad

KYET U SALAT YWET THOKE　ကြက်ဥဆလပ်ရွက်သုပ်

This is apparently the dish that my mother used to win the heart of my father.
They were at medical school together in Mandalay and she was the only one
out of the lot of them who could cook. Whenever the students went on a
group picnic, everyone insisted she made this egg salad. It's simple and light,
and gorgeous in a sandwich, or on toast (seriously).

Serves 4

1 round or butterhead lettuce
6 eggs
1 tablespoon Crispy Fried Onions
　(page 238) or shop-bought fried
　onions, to garnish

For the dressing
1 tablespoon groundnut oil or
　other neutral-tasting oil
2 tablespoons smooth or crunchy
　peanut butter
2 tablespoons fish sauce
juice of ½ lime
¼ teaspoon MSG or ½
　tablespoon chicken or
　vegetable bouillon

Mix the dressing ingredients together in a small bowl.

Separate the lettuce leaves, wash, drain thoroughly and tear each leaf in half.
Place the torn leaves in a large salad bowl.

Soft boil the eggs (see Cook's Note) and cool, peel and quarter them.

Drizzle the dressing all over the lettuce leaves and massage with your hands so
the leaves become coated and slightly wilted. Add the cooled soft-boiled egg
quarters and combine gently to avoid breaking them up.

Scatter the crispy fried onions on top and serve with plain rice or in a sandwich.

Cook's Note
For the perfect egg with a slightly fudgy yolk: place room temperature eggs
in a saucepan, cover in cold water and heat on high until the eggs start to boil
and bubble furiously. Immediately turn the heat down to medium and continue
to simmer for another 7 minutes. Remove from heat and submerge in cold,
running water to stop the eggs cooking.

Shredded Chicken & Tomato Salad

KYET THAR THOKE ကြက်သားသုပ်

This dish uses the most classic Burmese salad dressing. The key component is the gram flour (page 240), which is toasted to give a nutty, aromatic flavour. Try to find unripe tomatoes if you can, as these will provide more texture and a fresher, 'greener' note, which is common in Burmese salads. The salad can form a complete meal with rice and soup on the side or can be served as a starter. Burmese tomato salad is made the same way – simply swap the chicken for fried pulses such as chana dal or broad beans.

Serves 4
as a starter or side dish

For the salad
2 onions or 4 banana shallots, very thinly sliced (preferably using a mandoline)
4 skinless chicken thigh fillets
1 tablespoon sugar
1 teaspoon salt
2 tomatoes, sliced into strips (keeping the seeds), or 10 cherry tomatoes, quartered
2 green finger chillies, sliced into rings

For the dressing
2 tablespoons Toasted Gram Flour (page 240)
2 tablespoons fish sauce
4 tablespoons turmeric oil (page 118)
juice of ½ lime

For the garnish
handful of coriander leaves, torn
handful of shredded spring onions, green parts only (if serving as part of a meal)

Soak the onion slices in a small bowl of cold water. Leave until ready to serve the dish.

Place the chicken in a saucepan with the sugar, salt and 500ml of water. Bring to the boil over a high heat and immediately turn the heat down to medium. Simmer, uncovered, for 15 minutes, then remove the pan from the heat. Set to one side.

Remove the chicken from the stock (reserve the stock for another recipe) and slice into small strips. Add to a large bowl along with the tomatoes, chillies, and the ingredients for the dressing. Drain the onions and add these, then mix thoroughly, preferably by hand.

If serving the salad as part of a meal, reheat the stock until simmering, then ladle into four small bowls. Top with black pepper, shredded spring onions and half of the coriander leaves.

Divide the chicken salad between four small dishes, garnish with the remaining coriander leaves and serve immediately (with the soup and steaming white rice if desired).

Cook's Note
Soaking the onion removes the astringent 'raw' taste, but also keeps the slices crisp, which is important in this dish.

Burmese Tofu Salad

TOHU THOKE တိုဟူးသုပ်

Tofu salad, I hear you cry? Before you start turning the page, you should know that this stuff is the bomb! Make the recipe for chickpea tofu (Burmese Tofu Fritters, page 44), fry half of it into the best little snacks you will ever eat, and turn the other half into this wonderful, punchy salad, which is great as part of a meal or for those in-between moments. In Yangon, tamarind is used for sharpness, but in Mandalay vinegar is preferred.

Serves 2-4
as a starter

250g slab of chickpea tofu (½ quantity recipe on page 44)

For the dressing
2 tablespoons malt vinegar
1 teaspoon light soy sauce
½ teaspoon dark soy sauce
½ teaspoon yellow soy bean sauce
½ teaspoon Chilli Oil (page 236)
6 garlic cloves, peeled and crushed

To garnish
1 tablespoon Fried Red-skin Peanuts (page 240) or salted peanuts, crushed
1 tablespoon Crispy Fried Onions (page 238) or shop-bought fried onions
small handful of coriander leaves, shredded

Slice the tofu into the shape of French fries and place in a mixing bowl. Add the dressing ingredients and toss together with your hands.

Dish up in a shallow bowl and sprinkle the garnishes on top, and serve as a snack or starter.

Fishcake Salad

NGA HPE THOKE ငါးဖယ်သုပ်

Though I am rather a fan of those bread-crumbed discs stuffed with fish and potato, the fishcake used in this salad is the squidgy Asian-style made from surimi or featherback fish known as *satsuma-age* in Japanese or *eomuk* in Korean. I actually prefer to use fish balls, which I find to have a more pleasingly bouncy texture. But both fish balls and fishcake can be found in the refrigerated section of Asian supermarkets. You can also use frozen varieties, simply defrost before using.

Serves 4

400g fresh or frozen ready-made
  Asian fishcake or fish balls
2 tablespoons groundnut oil or
  other neutral-tasting oil
6 white cabbage leaves,
  shredded
2 banana shallots, thinly sliced
1 tablespoon fish sauce
¼ teaspoon MSG or ½
  tablespoon chicken or
  vegetable bouillon
2 tablespoons Toasted Gram
  Flour (page 240)
juice of ½ lime

To garnish
1 tablespoon Crispy Noodles
  (page 239)
1 tablespoon Crispy Fried Onions
  (page 238) or shop-bought
  fried onions
handful of coriander leaves

Slice the fishcake or cut the fish balls into quarters.

Heat the oil in a wok or frying pan over a medium-high heat. Add the fishcake slices and shallow-fry in the oil for 5 minutes until slightly browned at the edges. Transfer to a large bowl along with the rest of the salad ingredients and mix well.

Divide the salad between four plates or bowls or serve on a platter for people to help themselves. Garnish with the crispy noodles (page 239), fried onions (page 238) and coriander leaves and serve.

Hand-tossed Rainbow Salad

LET THOKE SONE လက်သုပ်စုံ

Calling this triple-carb beauty a salad almost seems like an insult, as its vibrant flavours and textures make it as far from a droopy bunch of green leaves as you can possibly imagine. As it's served cold or at room temperature, it's always welcome at a barbecue, perfect picnic fare and it even makes a wonderful lunch *al desko*. Its name literally means 'hand-tossed everything', but it's so bright and cheerful that 'rainbow salad' seems much more appropriate.

In Burma, you'll see this sold by *gaun ywet thair* – ladies who walk along the streets carrying all the equipment and ingredients piled up on a tray on their head. If you call them over, they will gladly bring down and unwrap the packages that they've balanced so skilfully, and prepare you a fresh portion on the spot. You can ask them to leave out anything you're not keen on (e.g. carrots are rare and often Burmese people don't like them), or ask for more of another ingredient and they're always happy to oblige.

A variation of this dish is called *htamin thoke* (rice salad). Pretty much the only difference is there is no papaya in *htamin thoke* and there's a lot more rice.

Serves 4-6

200g dried mung bean
   thread noodles
200g basmati rice
1 tablespoon tomato purée
2 large potatoes, peeled
30g dried shrimp
4 teaspoons Shan Fermented
   Soybeans (page 241) or
   Japanese natto or miso
4 tablespoons Toasted Gram
   Flour (page 240)
4 white cabbage leaves, sliced
   into thin strips
2 large carrots, sliced into
   thin strips
¼ green papaya, peeled and
   sliced into thin strips (optional)
4 tablespoons groundnut oil or
   other neutral-tasting oil
4 teaspoons tamarind paste
   mixed with 4 tablespoons water
4 tablespoons fish sauce

...continued on page 78

Place the noodles in a heatproof bowl, pour over enough just-boiled water to submerge and leave to soak for 30 minutes. Drain and rinse with cold water. Set to one side.

Place the rice in a saucepan and add enough water so it reaches 2.5cm above the level of the rice (about the first knuckle joint if you use a clean index finger to touch the surface of the rice). Now add the tomato purée – this will tint the rice red and adds a hint of tomato flavour. Cover with a lid, bring to the boil and then immediately turn the heat down to low and steam for 20 minutes. The rice should be perfectly cooked by the end. Leave to cool and set to one side.

While the rice is cooking, cook the potatoes in a saucepan of boiling salted water until just tender. Drain and slice into fat discs, then set to one side.

Blitz the dried shrimp into a powdery fluff using a blender or food processor. All the ingredients should be at room temperature at this point.

Now the fun bit: get out a big salad bowl or mixing bowl and toss in the noodles, rice, potatoes, shrimp dust, soy beans and gram flour. Add the cabbage, carrots and papaya. Add the groundnut oil, tamarind and fish sauce and mix lightly together using your hands.

...continued on page 78

To garnish

handful of Fried Red-skin
  Peanuts (page 240)
handful of coriander leaves,
  chopped
Crispy Fried Onions (page 238)
  or shop-bought fried onions
Chilli Oil (page 236) or shop-
  bought chilli oil

Serve immediately, sprinkled with the garnishes, or keep, covered, for a few hours in the fridge or in a sealed container in a cool bag and scatter over the garnishes just before serving.

Cook's Note

You can serve this dish two ways – either ready-mixed on a platter or with all the ingredients in small dishes for diners to help themselves. It's much more fun to DIY though. The Burmese actually prefer to adjust flavours at the table according to their own personal taste – a bit more salt here, or a bit more sourness there – and here, I'd recommend getting stuck right in yourself. Remember it's called 'hand-tossed everything'!

Pickled Ginger & Sesame Salad

GIN THOKE   ချင်းသုပ်

This is probably the second most famous Burmese salad after *lahpet thoke* and shares a lot of the same ingredients, although note that this time the tomato used in the salad should definitely be green if possible. In Burma, ginger salad is particularly popular with women, as apparently it helps with menstrual cramps! The salad is usually made using fresh ginger that you've sliced as thinly as possible and lightly pickled yourself, but it's so much easier to pick up a jar of pickled ginger shreds. which is widely available these days. I particularly like the 'Very Lazy' brand though most supermarkets have their own version, and the Japanese ginger known as *kizami shoga* also works very well.

Serves 2–4
as a snack or side dish

1 tablespoon dried shrimp
40g pickled shredded ginger
  (such as Japanese *kizami
  beni shoga*)
1 tablespoon roasted peas or
  roasted chana dal (daria dal)
  (such as Hodmedod's)
1 tablespoon fried broad beans
1 tablespoon Fried Red-skin
  Peanuts (page 240) or shop-
  bought salted peanuts
1 tablespoon Crispy Fried Garlic
  (page 238) or shop-bought
  fried garlic
1 teaspoon toasted sesame
  seeds
1 teaspoon Toasted Gram Flour
  (see page 240)
1 green finger chilli, sliced
  into rings
½ medium unripe (green or
  yellow) tomato, sliced
juice of ¼ lime
1 tablespoon groundnut oil or
  other neutral-tasting oil
½ teaspoon fish sauce

Blitz or pound the dried shrimp to a pulp using a food processor or mortar and pestle. Tip into a bowl and mix with the rest of the ingredients. Serve as a snack or side dish.

Soups

HIN GYO

ဟင်းချို

Soup is never a starter in Burma – instead it's a lubricant. With every meal, in lieu of a drink, we serve a light broth or consomme called *hin gyo* or, if it's sour, *chinyay hin*, which is served from communal bowls with several china spoons attached, so you can sip from them delicately or ladle straight into your own dish.

And since no meal is complete without a bowl of soup, variety is necessary, but whether it's soothing, sour or peppery, it always slips down with ease.

Bottle Gourd & Glass Noodle Soup

BUTHI HIN GYO   ဘူးသီးဟင်းချို

Have fun fighting over the slippery noodles and chunks of gourd that bob
about in this peppery soup. It goes particularly well as a side to any meat or
chicken curry, and can easily be made vegetarian by swapping the shrimp
and shrimp paste for a tablespoon of vegetable bouillon or Japanese miso.

Serves 4

1 tablespoon groundnut oil or
    other neutral-tasting oil
6 dried shrimp
½ onion, sliced
3 garlic cloves, halved
400g bottle gourd (*dudhi*),
    peeled and sliced into 2cm
    width crescents
25g dried mung bean thread
    noodles (about a small handful)
1 teaspoon shrimp paste
    (*belacan*)
1 teaspoon salt
freshly ground black pepper

Heat the oil in a medium saucepan over a medium-high heat. Add the dried
shrimp and fry for 5 minutes, until fragrant. Now add the onion and garlic and
fry for another 5 minutes until they begin to turn translucent.

Pour in 1 litre of boiling water from the kettle and add the bottle gourd, noodles,
shrimp paste and salt. Simmer for 20 minutes, add a grind of black pepper and
then serve with a curry dish and rice.

Cook's Note
It works equally well to substitute cucumber or chayote for the bottle gourd
in this recipe – just halve the cooking time for cucumber to avoid it turning
into mush.

Shrimp & Cabbage Soup

BALAR HIN GYO ပလာဟင်းချို

Although cabbage soup may make you think of poor old Charlie Bucket in Roald Dahl's *Charlie and the Chocolate Factory*, the white variety of cabbage is actually rather sweet and fragrant, and combined with equally sweet dried shrimp, it makes a surprisingly satisfying concoction. This soup is often the default for any meal as it can be made very quickly and goes with pretty much everything.

Serves 4–6
as a side dish

1 tablespoon groundnut oil
   or other neutral-tasting oil
12 dried shrimp
½ medium onion, sliced
3 garlic cloves, halved
6 white cabbage leaves,
   tough stalks removed
   and leaves quartered
1 teaspoon shrimp paste
   (*belacan*)
1 teaspoon salt
freshly ground black pepper

Heat the oil in a saucepan over a medium-high heat. Add the dried shrimp and fry for 5 minutes, until fragrant. Now add the onion and garlic and fry for another 5 minutes, until they begin to turn translucent.

Pour in 1 litre of boiling water from the kettle, then add the cabbage, shrimp paste, salt and plenty of pepper. Simmer for 20 minutes and then serve with a curry dish and rice.

Classic Sour Soup

CHINYAY HIN

This soup is one that I loved growing up and still request whenever I have dinner with my parents. I have been known to eat a big bowl of plain rice swimming in this soup and nothing else. *Chinyay* means 'sour water' and this is usually achieved using tamarind, but my family have always favoured lime juice, so that's the version I present to you here.

Theezohn chinyay (rainbow vegetable sour soup) is a more lavish version of this soup that's served on special occasions. To make it, add some green beans, a chopped carrot, a chopped drumstick vegetable (*Moringa oleifera*), two boiled eggs and a pinch of garam masala, and simmer until the vegetables are cooked through.

Serves 6
as a side dish

2 medium onions, peeled
1 spring onion, green and
   white parts
1 small ripe tomato, roughly
   chopped
1cm piece of ginger, peeled
2 garlic cloves, peeled
2 tablespoons groundnut oil
   or other neutral-tasting oil
pinch of ground turmeric
1 teaspoon shrimp paste
   (*belacan*)
1 tablespoon dried shrimp
1 tablespoon rice flour
6cm piece of daikon (mooli),
   sliced, or 8 radishes, trimmed
100g spinach leaves
3 tablespoons fish sauce
juice of ½ lime

Slice one onion and set to one side. Roughly chop the other onion and blitz it with the spring onion, tomato, ginger and garlic in a blender to a smooth paste.

Heat the oil in a saucepan over a high heat. Add the turmeric to the oil and allow to sizzle for a few seconds. Now turn the heat down to medium and add the onion paste, then fry for 10 minutes until fragrant and darkened. Add the shrimp paste, dried shrimp and rice flour, and fry for another 3–4 minutes.

Pour in 750ml of water, turn the heat to high and bring to the boil. Turn the heat back down to medium and simmer for 5 minutes and then add the reserved sliced onion, daikon and spinach. Simmer for another 20 minutes, until the onion and daikon are soft and translucent and the spinach dark and wilted.

Stir in the fish sauce and lime juice and ladle between bowls. Serve with Chinese soup spoons, as a side to a curry with rice.

Cook's Note
You can substitute the tomato with the juice from a 400g tin of plum tomatoes or 2 tablespoons of tomato purée.

Bean soup

PE HIN GYO   ပဲဟင်းချို

This is a rustic, textured soup that is more akin to a *dal*. Favoured by children for its soothing nature, it's eaten as part of a main meal (as with the rest of our soups) but, being thicker than most, it's just as likely to be spooned onto rice as drunk straight from the bowl. Mung bean thread noodles are often added to this soup to make it heartier – just add a handful of the dried noodles at the same time as the lentils and water.

Serves 4-6

150g dried red lentils or yellow
  split peas
2 tablespoons groundnut oil
  or other neutral-tasting oil
2 medium onions, peeled
  and sliced
1 garlic cloves, peeled and sliced
1 teaspoon salt
Crispy Fried Onions (page 238)
  or shop-bought fried onions,
  to garnish

If using the yellow split peas, soak in plenty of water overnight. Skip this step if using red lentils.

Heat the oil in a large saucepan over a medium-high heat. Add the onions and garlic and fry for 3 minutes, until fragrant. Now add the lentils or yellow split peas (if they were soaked, drain them first), stir and then add the salt and 1.25 litres of water.

Turn the heat up to high and bring to the boil (watch in case it boils over), reduce the heat to medium-low and simmer for 30 minutes, stirring occasionally, until the lentils break down (if using red lentils, these will turn yellow). Serve in individual bowls, garnished with crispy onions.

Rice

HTAMIN

ထမင်း

Rice is life in Burma. It's how we say, 'Hello!' as we ask, 'Have you had your rice yet?'. Burma was once known as the rice bowl of Asia, as, before World War II, it was the world's largest exporter of rice and it is still the sixth largest.

Even now, the Irrawaddy delta is devoted to paddy fields and the Burmese will often feel like something's amiss if they go for one meal, let alone one day, without rice.

Plain rice is loved best, as even your everyday meal in Burma involves a spread of dishes, which complement that bowl of rice, but we like to have Golden Sticky Rice (page 97) for breakfast and on special occasions we will have Shan Sour Rice (page 102) or even indulge in our own elaborate take on biryani (page 98).

Buttered Lentil Rice

PE HTAWBAT HTAMIN   ပဲေထာပတ်ထမင်း

This is a very simple but delicious rice, which makes an excellent foil for richer curries, especially ones with an Indian influence such as Burmese Masala Chicken (page 151), Goat and Split Pea Curry (page 138) and Golden Pumpkin Curry (page 187). The recipe makes quite a modest portion (for once) so feel free to double the quantities, depending on how hungry you are!

Serves 4
as a side dish

50g dried red lentils, chana dal
  or yellow split peas
220g basmati rice, rinsed
  and drained
2 tablespoons salted butter
2 bay leaves
2 cloves
1 teaspoon salt
½ teaspoon sugar

Soak the lentils in a large bowl of water overnight. The next day, rinse and drain the lentils. Place both the lentils and the rice in a saucepan with the rest of the ingredients along with 400ml of fresh water.

Cover the pan with a lid and bring to the boil over a high heat. Turn the heat to low and simmer for 20 minutes or until the lentils are soft and the rice is cooked.

Leave to stand for 5 minutes and then serve with a hearty meat curry such as the braised beef curry (page 134) or goat and split pea curry (page 138).

Golden Sticky Rice

SEE-HTAMIN ဆီထမင်း

Traditionally served with Sprouted Yellow Peas and Onions (page 179) or fried dried fish, this fragrant sticky rice is so compelling that I find it difficult to put my spoon down. *See-htamin* literally means 'oiled rice' but this is an inadequate name for such splendour. Join me in my addiction as you scrape forlornly at the last few caramelised grains at the bottom of the pan.

Serves 6–8

200g glutinous rice
90ml groundnut oil or other
   neutral-tasting oil
2 onions, sliced thinly
¼ teaspoon ground turmeric
1 teaspoon salt
¼ teaspoon MSG or ½
   tablespoon chicken or
   vegetable bouillon

Place the rice in a bowl with plenty of water and set to one side to soak for 1 hour. Drain thoroughly.

Heat the oil in a large saucepan over a medium heat, and add the onions and turmeric. Toss and fry for 5 minutes or until the onions are soft and starting to brown a little. Add the rice, salt and MSG, and stir. Flatten the rice with a spatula or the palm of your hand so it forms an even layer in the pan, then pour in 230ml of water. Cover the pan with a lid and bring to the boil. Turn the heat to low and cook for 40 minutes. It's okay if the rice sticks to the bottom of the pan a little. The crust that forms is prized by many.

Turn off the heat and leave to rest for 5 minutes before serving with sprouted yellow peas with fried onion (page 179), crispy shrimp relish (page 212) or *balachaung* (page 211).

Burmese 'Biryani'

DANBAUK   ဒန်ပေါက်

There are two types of Burmese 'biryani' or *danbauk*, and both of them are usually served at celebrations and other formal occasions. The first type is known as *theezohn danbauk* ('rainbow vegetable *danbauk*') – with a curried sauce and packed with vegetables such as peas and carrots, it is much more recognisable as a biryani dish, and is popular in Yangon. This recipe is for the second type known as *a-sein danbauk* ('fresh *danbauk*'), which is more popular in Mandalay. A fragrant chicken pilaf, this dish bears a much greater resemblance to Persian cooking – in fact the name *danbauk* is derived from the Persian culinary term *dum pukht*. *A-sein danbauk* was served at my own wedding in Burma, and I will always associate it with happiness, festivity and largesse.

    Both types of *danbauk* are served with a spread of fresh chillies, fresh mint, Crispy Shrimp Relish (page 212) and a sour soup made with roselle (just add a handful of roselle or sorrel leaves to some chicken stock), all of which help balance the buttery richness of the rice. *Theezohn danbauk* is also served with Indian-style mango pickle, as befits its Indian influences, whereas *a-sein danbauk* is served with Burmese coleslaw. Whenever I make this at home, everyone asks for seconds.

Serves 8

1.25kg skinless chicken thighs
650g basmati rice, uncooked
1 tablespoon ground cinnamon
1 tablespoon sugar
125g salted butter, softened
100ml plain yoghurt

For the rice spices
handful of cashews
handful of raisins
16 cardamom pods
4–5 bay leaves
2 cinnamon sticks
6 cloves
few strands of saffron (optional)

For the chicken marinade
2 tablespoons sugar
1 tablespoon ground cinnamon
2 tablespoons Crispy Fried
   Onions (page 238) or shop-
   bought fried onions
1 chicken stock cube
125g salted butter, softened

Place the rice spices in a large bowl and add 200ml of warm water. Leave to soak for 1 hour.

Place the chicken in a large lidded casserole pan that can be used on the hob.

Add the ingredients for the marinade along with 50ml of water and rub all over the chicken. Set to one side for 15 minutes.

Next, place the pan on the hob, covered, over a high heat. Bring to the boil, reduce the heat to medium and simmer for about 10 minutes. Check that the chicken is cooked through and then remove to a plate or chopping board. Wrap in foil to keep warm and set to one side, reserving the stock in the pan.

Add the rice to the reserved stock, and pour in the water from the soaked spices, leaving the spices behind in the bowl.

Top up the water in the pan so it reaches 2.5cm above the level of the rice (about your first knuckle joint if you use a clean index finger to touch the surface of the rice). Now add the cinnamon, sugar, butter, yoghurt and all the soaked spices. Cover, bring to the boil and then immediately turn the heat down to low. Allow the rice to steam with the lid still on for 20 minutes. Remove the lid and return the chicken

To serve

Burmese Coleslaw (page 242)

roselle soup (see recipe
    introduction) or Classic Sour
    Soup (page 88)

Crispy Shrimp Relish (page 212)

finger chillies

mint leaves

to the pan. Mix through gently to combine the rice and chicken and then it's ready to serve.

Serve each plate of *danbauk* with Burmese coleslaw (page 242), roselle soup, crispy shrimp relish (page 212), fresh finger chillies and fresh mint leaves.

Rice is an essential throughout Burma, and is sold by the sack or scooped into plastic bags.

Shan Sour Rice

HTAMIN CHIN ထမင်းချဉ်

When I was 18, I went to Burma without my parents for the first time. I stayed with one of my aunts, and one morning she said to me, 'I'm going to make *htamin chin* for lunch today. Do you want it made with fish or potato?' Surprised, I said, 'Eh, Mum makes it with both' and my aunt gave me a long look and then said, 'Your Mum spoils you'. Note that in Burmese this was even more scathing, as use of 'your Mum' rather than 'my sister' is quite pointed.

Anyway, here I am spoiling you too with this recipe for Shan Sour Rice – tomato and tamarind rice balls mixed with fish *and* potato and all sorts of other tasty titbits, including lashings of garlic. Incidentally, the way that it's shown in the photo is how another aunt likes to serve it at her parties. The lacquered basket was actually her wedding present to me.

The rice balls should be accompanied by the pictured discs of Shan Fermented Soybeans (page 241) and garlic chive roots (known as *juu myit*), but, hey, we all have to draw the line somewhere…

Makes 6 generous rice balls

2 medium potatoes (about 400g)
150g white fish fillet, such as cod or pollock
320g jasmine rice
¼ teaspoon ground turmeric
juice only from 400g tin tomatoes or 3 tablespoons tomato purée
90ml 'Cooked' Oil (page 239)
2 tablespoons Shan Fermented Soy Beans (page 241) or Japanese *natto* or miso
2 tablespoons tamarind paste
1 tablespoon fish sauce

To serve
4 spring onions, green parts only, shredded
handful of coriander leaves, shredded
Crispy Fried Onions (page 238) or shop-bought fried onions
Crispy Fried Garlic (page 238) or shop-bought fried garlic
Fried Red-skin Peanuts (page 240) or salted peanuts
6 garlic cloves, peeled
Chilli Oil (page 236)
Bottle Gourd and Glass Noodle Soup (page 84)
prawn crackers or decent potato crisps

Quarter the potatoes and place them in a saucepan with water and bring to the boil. Cook until completely soft and then drain. When cool enough to handle, peel. Set to one side.

Using clean hands, squeeze the fish over a sink to get rid of as much moisture as possible and set to one side.

Place the rice in a large saucepan, sprinkle over the turmeric and add the tomato juice to the pan. Top up with water so it reaches 2.5cm above the level of the rice (about your first knuckle joint if using a clean index finger to touch the surface of the rice).

Cover the pan with a lid, bring to the boil over a high heat and then immediately turn the heat down to low. Uncover the pan, place the fish on top of the rice, put the lid back on and steam for 20 minutes. The rice (and fish) should be perfectly cooked by the end of the cooking time.

Add the cooked potatoes to the pan. As soon as the rice is cool enough to touch, use your hands to knead the rice, fish and potatoes together until the mixture becomes slightly sticky. Add the cooked oil, bean and tamarind pastes and the fish sauce, and knead again.

Form the mixture into six generous balls and put into six shallow bowls or dishes. Make an indentation in each ball and top with spring onions, coriander leaves, crispy fried onions and garlic and fried red-skin peanuts. Place a garlic clove on each dish and then serve with the chilli oil, bottle gourd and noodle soup and crackers on the side for people to help themselves.

Noodles

MONT DI, KHAO SWÈ

မုန့်တီ, ခေါက်ဆွဲ

There is a Burmese saying that a marriage will not work if one party likes noodles and the other likes rice. Although the national dish of Burma is a noodle dish called *mohinga* (Fish Noodle Soup, page 107), the noodles are made of rice, which makes for a happy compromise.

As well as *mohinga*, many of the most renowned Burmese dishes are noodle-based such as *ohn-no khao swè*, the cousin of the Thai *khao soi*, *Shan khao swè* i.e. Shan noodles, and *Mandalay mont di* – a fat noodle salad from the old capital of Burma. Many of the following dishes are only available at breakfast or lunchtime in Burma, but despite this they all make excellent dinner party food, especially when accompanied by various fritters.

Fish Noodle Soup, Burma's National Dish

MOHINGA

မုန့်ဟင်းခါး

Bursting with contrasting textures, fragrances and flavours, *mohinga* is a catfish noodle soup served over rice vermicelli. It's the breakfast of choice wherever you go in Burma, and considered our national dish.

As soon as we wake up in Yangon, my family and I will devour bowl after bowl of *mohinga*, brought to us in huge metal tiffin carriers from the nearest street vendor, or eaten in situ at our favourite stall.

Heaped with crispy Split Pea Crackers (page 50), slices of soft duck egg, bouncy fishcake and fresh feathery coriander, with lashings of chilli oil, fish sauce and lime on the side, it's hard to know when to stop, and for many, their love for *mohinga* borders on obsession.

Serves 6-8

200g dried rice vermicelli
noodles
8 tablespoons groundnut oil or
other neutral-tasting oil
200g ready-made Asian-style
fishcake, sliced
5 tablespoons gram flour
2 tablespoons rice flour
200g tinned mackerel in brine
100g tinned sardines in oil
handful of sliced banana
stem or shredded banana
blossom (optional)
500ml fish stock
6 shallots or small onions,
trimmed
2 tablespoons fish sauce

For the spice paste
4 garlic cloves, peeled
3cm piece of ginger, peeled
2 lemongrass stalks, trimmed
of woody bits
small bunch of coriander stems
(reserve leaves for serving)
1 tablespoon mild chilli powder
1 tablespoon ground turmeric
1 teaspoon paprika
1 teaspoon freshly ground
black pepper

Place the noodles into a heatproof bowl or container and submerge with just-boiled water. Untangle them with chopsticks or a fork, then leave to soak for 15 minutes. Drain in a colander and rinse thoroughly with cold running water. Set to one side in the colander so they can continue to drain.

Heat 2 tablespoons of oil in a wok or frying pan over a medium heat. Add the fishcake slices and stir-fry for 5 minutes, until golden at the edges. Set to one side.

Sift the flours together into a bowl. Heat a dry frying pan (i.e. no oil or water) over a medium heat. Add the flours in an even layer and toast them for 3–4 minutes until fragrant. Make sure you toss the flours gently and keep moving the pan to avoid it catching and burning – the flours can blacken in seconds.

Leave the flours to cool and then tip back into the bowl. Slowly add 500ml of cold water while whisking to combine. Set this flour solution to one side.

Next make the spice paste. Blitz the garlic, ginger, lemongrass and coriander stems in a food processor or blender to a smooth paste. Heat the remaining 6 tablespoons of oil in a stockpot over a medium-high heat, add the paste and the rest of the spices and stir-fry for 3–4 minutes, until fragrant.

Add the tinned fish to the stockpot along with their oil and brine. Use a potato masher or a fork to mash the fish until smooth and stir to combine with the spice paste. Now add the banana stem or blossom, if using, the flour solution and stock, stir well and bring to the boil. Reduce the heat to medium and simmer vigorously for 30 minutes.

...continued on page 108

...continued on page 108

To serve

Split Pea Crackers (page 50)

2 white cabbage leaves, shredded

4 hard-boiled eggs, peeled and cut into wedges

2 limes, cut into wedges

fish sauce

Crispy Fried Onions (page 238) or shop-bought fried onions

Crispy Fried Garlic (page 238) or shop-bought fried garlic

Chilli Oil (page 236)

Add another 2 litres of water, reduce the heat to low and simmer the broth for a further 1½ hours. By now, the broth should be the colour of brown mustard, and the consistency of French onion soup (i.e. not as thick as a dal nor as thin as consommé). Add the shallots and simmer for another 30 minutes. They will soften and turn translucent but should remain whole.

When ready to serve, stir the 2 tablespoons of fish sauce into the broth. Divide the noodles between shallow bowls and ladle enough broth over the top so that the noodles are almost completely submerged. Garnish with the fishcake, shards of split pea cracker, shredded cabbage, egg and chopped coriander leaves. Serve with soup spoons, or ideally metal Chinese/Thai soup spoons, with the lime wedges, fish sauce, crispy fried onions and garlic and chilli oil on the side.

Cook's Note

Mohinga is usually made with small river catfish known in Burmese as *nga gyi*, *nga ku* and *nga yunt*, but a combination of tinned mackerel and sardines somehow successfully matches the flavour of authentic *mohinga* better than any other fish I've found in the UK. My father said to me, in slightly unnecessary surprise, 'This tastes just like the real thing'.

The Burmese actually call metal Chinese/Thai spoons *mohinga zun* or 'mohinga spoons' – please never serve *mohinga* with chopsticks as, essentially, it is a soup that just happens to have some noodles in it – much like minestrone.

Many *mohinga* vendors and stalls will offer *like bwe* for free – literally meaning a chaser plate, it's an extra ladleful of broth (but not noodles).

Coconut Chicken Noodles

OHN-NO KHAO SWÈ   အုန်းနို့ခေါက်ဆွဲ

This wonderfully subtle dish is our take on *laksa* – so comforting and flavoursome I like to call it a 'hug in a bowl'. Ironically, it may well be our most famous export, as it's a cousin to the northern Thai *khao soi* – a dish so beloved that it has spawned its own fan sites and even essays – and in the rest of Asia *ohn-no khao swè* is known as *khao sway*, *khauk swe* and my absolute favourite, *cow suey*. *Ohn-no khao swè* literally means 'coconut milk noodles' (and then you get into all kinds of murky cultural metonymy, as *no* or *note* not only means 'milk' but also 'breast' in Burmese), but the usual protein is chicken, hence my paraphrase of coconut chicken noodles.

Serves 4–6

250g dried egg or wheat noodles
5 tablespoons groundnut oil or
   other neutral-tasting oil
3 medium onions, finely chopped
1cm piece of ginger, peeled
4 garlic cloves, peeled
2 spring onions, roughly chopped
2 tablespoons gram flour
2 tablespoons fish sauce
¼ teaspoon MSG or ½
   tablespoon chicken bouillon
500g skinless chicken thigh
   fillets, cut into small strips
2 tablespoons paprika
200ml coconut milk

To serve
2 banana shallots or 1 red onion,
   sliced very thinly, soaked in
   cold water
2 hard-boiled eggs, peeled and
   sliced into rounds
Crispy Noodles (page 239)
fish sauce
Chilli Oil (page 236)
2 limes, cut into wedges

Cook the noodles according to the packet instructions. Drain in a colander and rinse thoroughly under cold running water, then set to one side in the colander so that any residual water can continue to drain.

Heat 2 tablespoons of oil in a large saucepan or stockpot over a medium-low heat, add the onions and fry for 10 minutes until soft and translucent. Take a tablespoonful of the fried onions out of the pan and place in the bowl of a food processor or blender. Add the ginger, garlic and spring onions to the food processor, then blitz together to form a rough paste. Set to one side.

Place the flour in a jug or bowl and slowly whisk in 100ml of cold water. Add to the pan of fried onions along with the fish sauce and MSG. Bring to a simmer over a medium heat, then top up with 500ml of cold water. Bring the broth back to a simmer, then keep simmering while you prepare everything else.

Heat the remaining 3 tablespoons of oil in a wok or frying pan, add the ginger-garlic paste and stir-fry over a high heat for a couple of minutes. Add the chicken strips and 1 tablespoon of paprika, toss to combine and stir-fry for about 5 minutes, until the chicken is cooked and browned.

Gently stir the coconut milk and the remaining tablespoon of paprika into the pan of simmering broth. Add the stir-fried chicken, bring back to the simmer over a medium heat and cook for 15 minutes. At this stage the broth can be cooled, covered and kept in the fridge for 24 hours or frozen, if you like (see Cook's Note).

When you're ready to serve, thoroughly drain the shallots.

...continued on page 110

Divide the cooked noodles between pasta bowls, then ladle enough hot chicken broth over to cover. Fan the shallot and egg slices over the top and scatter with the crispy noodles. Add another dash of fish sauce to each serving and have some chilli oil on the side and wedges of lime for squeezing. Serve with metal Chinese/Thai spoons or soup spoons (but never chopsticks).

Cook's Note
The chicken broth freezes well and can be kept for up to 1 month. Thaw, then warm gently over a medium-low heat until piping hot.

Wood Ear & Glass Noodle Soup

KYA ZAN HIN ကြာဆံဟင်း

Even though the journey entailed a precarious six-hour drive from Mandalay up an unmade mountain path, I always looked forward to visiting my mother's family in Mogok, partly because our usual pit stop was a village called Shwenyaungbin where they plied us with sticky rice, all manner of fried things and *kya zan hin* (aka *kya zan chet*), an earthy noodle soup that warmed us inside and out – a necessity as the higher we travelled the chillier it became. For a heartier dish, we'll use sliced chicken instead of dried shrimp, and if you like the sound of this, make sure you use dark chicken meat, which will impart the right level of sweetness to the broth.

Serves 4

400g dried mung bean
   thread noodles

For the soup
15g dried lily flowers
15g dried wood-ear mushrooms
   (*kikurage*)
15g dried shrimp
50g dried tofu knots (optional)
6 shallots or small onions, peeled
   and trimmed
8 garlic cloves, peeled
juice from 400g tin of tomatoes or
   2 tablespoons tomato purée
¼ teaspoon MSG or ½
   tablespoon chicken or
   vegetable bouillon
200g ready-made Asian-style
   fish balls, halved
2 tablespoons fish sauce

To garnish
4 duck or hen's eggs or 12 quail
   eggs, hard-boiled and peeled
2 banana shallots or red onions,
   shaved thinly, soaked in
   cold water
handful of coriander leaves,
   chopped
2 limes, cut into wedges
Chilli Oil (page 236) or chilli flakes

Tie the lily flowers into knots and place them in a large heatproof bowl with the mushrooms, bearing in mind that both will expand greatly. Submerge in just-boiled water and leave to soak for 30 minutes until soft. Do not drain, but use scissors to snip the mushrooms into smaller pieces. Set to one side.

Heat a dry frying pan (i.e. no oil or water) over a high heat. Add the shrimp and toast by tossing for 8–10 minutes until charred, blackened and smelling smoky. Tip into a stockpot, then add the dried tofu knots (if using), the shallots, garlic, tomato juice or purée and 1 litre of water. Bring to the boil over a high heat, then reduce the heat to medium and simmer for 1 hour.

Add the mushrooms and lily flowers (including their soaking water) to the soup. Pour in another 1 litre of water, then add the MSG and fish balls. Bring the soup back to the boil over a high heat, then reduce the heat to medium and simmer for 15 minutes.

Add the noodles and immediately remove the pot from the stove – the noodles will cook in the residual heat.

If using duck or hen's eggs, slice them or cut into wedges. If using quail eggs, leave them whole.

When you're ready to serve, thoroughly drain the shaved shallots. Bring the *kya zan hin* back to the boil, add the fish sauce and stir through. Dish up the *kya zan hin* into shallow bowls, making sure each bowl has a bit of everything. Garnish with the eggs, shaved shallots and coriander leaves. Serve with metal Chinese/Thai spoons, or soup spoons (but never chopsticks), with lime wedges and chilli oil on the side for people to help themselves.

Shan Noodles

SHAN KHAO SWÈ　　ရှမ်းခေါက်ဆွဲ

As Burma is made up of 130 different ethnic groups, it means many of us can lay claim to a number of different cultures and cuisines. A large part of me is Shan, so I consider this dish from the mountainous Shan State as one of my heritage recipes. I like to make Shan noodles with a tomatoey sauce, while others prefer a clearer broth, but it should always be rich, savoury and sweet. Some people like to garnish their Shan noodles with crispy pork rinds (the airy type known as *chicharron* rather than pork scratchings) and crushed peanuts, or Fried Red-skin Peanuts (page 240), which add another crunchy dimension, but I usually serve mine topped with Burmese Tofu Fritters (page 44).

Serves 4

For the noodles
small bunch of spring onions
4 garlic cloves, peeled
4 ripe tomatoes or 200g tinned
　plum tomatoes
4 tablespoons groundnut oil or
　neutral-tasting oil
15g dried shrimp
400g minced pork or chicken
　(ideally thigh meat), or a 50:50 mix
1 tablespoon ground white pepper
1 tablespoon fish sauce
1 teaspoon caster sugar
1 tablespoon paprika
1 teaspoon mild chilli powder
400g dried narrow, flat rice noodles

To serve
4 tablespoons 'Cooked' Oil
　(page 239)
preserved mustard greens,
　chopped (available from Asian
　supermarkets)
handful of coriander leaves,
　shredded
Thai- or Filipino-style pork
　rinds (optional)
4 tablespoons Fried Red-skin
　Peanuts (optional) (page 240)
Burmese Coleslaw (page 242)
　(optional)
Burmese Tofu Fritters (page 44)
　(optional)
Chilli Oil (page 236)

Shred the green parts of the spring onions and set to one side. Trim the spring onion bulbs and put these and the white parts of the spring onions in a blender or food processor. Add the garlic and tomatoes to the blender and blitz to a smooth paste.

Heat 2 tablespoons of the oil in a large saucepan over a high heat and sauté the paste for 5 minutes until it starts to smell fragrant. Set to one side.

Heat a dry frying pan (i.e. no oil or water) over a high heat. Add the shrimp and toast by tossing for 8–10 minutes, until charred, blackened and smelling smoky. Turn the heat down to medium and add the remaining 2 tablespoons of oil along with the mince. Fry for another 10 minutes, breaking up any clumps, until the mince is browned. Add this mince and shrimp mix to the pan with the paste. Mix well and then add the pepper, fish sauce, sugar, paprika, chilli powder and 1 litre of water. Mix again, bring to the boil, then simmer for 20 minutes.

Meanwhile, put the noodles in a large heatproof bowl and submerge with just-boiled water. After a minute, untangle the noodles, then leave to soak for another 8–10 minutes. Drain in a colander and rinse thoroughly under cold running water. Set to one side in the colander to allow the noodles to continue to drain.

When you're ready to serve, reheat the noodles by placing the colander in your sink and pouring a kettleful of boiling water over them. Divide the noodles between four bowls and add a generous ladleful of the meat sauce and a tablespoon of the 'cooked' oil to each bowl.

Top with mustard greens, spring onion greens and shredded coriander leaves. Add a couple of pork rinds and a teaspoon of peanuts to each bowl if using. Serve immediately, with chopsticks and metal Chinese/Thai spoons and Burmese coleslaw, Burmese tofu fritters and chilli oil on the side for people to help themselves.

Mandalay Chicken Noodle Salad

MANDALAY MONT DI/NAN GYI THOKE   မန္တလေးမုန့်တီ / နန်းကြီးသုပ်

This delightful chicken noodle salad is a popular street food originally from Mandalay. Its proper name is *nan gyi mont di* or *nan gyi thoke* – *nan gyi* means 'gauge big' – but in Yangon, it is also known as *Mandalay mont di*. The actual (rice) noodle used is a little thinner than Japanese udon, but udon are a good substitute as long as you don't overcook them. Note that at some Burmese stalls and cafes, you can request a different thickness to your noodles by asking for *nan latt thoke*, which means 'gauge middle salad' and *nan thay thoke* which means 'gauge little salad'. There's even a variant made with flat wheat noodles similar to tagliatelle called *nan-byar-gyi khao swè* or *nan-byar-gyi thoke* (*byar* means 'flat').

The dish is usually mixed by hand, and then eaten by hand or using a spoon, but you'd be forgiven for a fork or chopsticks, and it's usually served with Mandalay Black Gram Fritters (page 54), Burmese Tofu Fritters (page 44) or Crispy Noodles (page 239).

Serves 4

400g dried udon noodles or
    dried tagliatelle
¼ bunch of coriander
freshly ground black pepper

For the chicken broth
500g chicken drumsticks or
    thighs, bone in and skin on
2 garlic cloves, peeled
1 teaspoon caster sugar
¼ teaspoon MSG or ½
    tablespoon chicken bouillon

For the chicken sauce
3 tablespoons groundnut oil
    or other neutral-tasting oil
3 medium onions, chopped
¼ teaspoon MSG or ½
    tablespoon chicken bouillon
2 tablespoons ground turmeric
2 tablespoons paprika
1 teaspoon hot chilli powder
freshly ground black pepper

…continued on page 118

If using dried udon noodles, half-fill a medium saucepan with water and bring to the boil. Scatter the noodles into the water, then immediately reduce the heat to medium-low and simmer for 15 minutes. Drain the noodles in a colander set in the sink. Run cold water over the noodles while you rub and swish them with your hand to rinse them. Set to one side.

If using tagliatelle, cook according to the packet instructions until al dente. Drain in a colander and rinse thoroughly with cold water, then set to one side in the colander so they can continue to drain.

Use a mortar and pestle to grind the coriander stems to a paste, or finely chop by hand. Roughly chop the coriander leaves. Set both to one side.

Put the chicken, coriander stem paste, garlic, sugar and ¼ teaspoon of MSG in a large saucepan with 1 litre of water. Bring to the boil, then reduce the heat to medium-low and simmer for 1 hour, skimming any scum that rises from the surface. Remove the chicken, take the meat off the bone in large strips and set to one side (discard the skin and bones). Keep the broth warm.

To make the sauce, heat the oil in another saucepan over a high heat. Add the onions and stir-fry for 3 minutes until fragrant. Reduce the heat to medium-low and add ¼ teaspoon of MSG, the turmeric, paprika and chilli powder, and 100ml of water. Mix thoroughly and cook gently, stirring occasionally, for 1–2 hours until the onions have broken down completely and the sauce turns a rich, caramelised brown. If it looks like the onions might stick and burn at any

…continued on page 118

For the turmeric oil

2 tablespoons ground turmeric

4 tablespoons groundnut oil or
  other neutral-tasting oil

For the garnishes

2 tablespoons groundnut oil or
  other neutral-tasting oil

200g ready-made Asian-style
  fishcake, sliced

2 banana shallots or red onions,
  shaved thinly, soaked in
  cold water

4 tablespoons Toasted Gram
  Flour (page 240)

4 tablespoons fish sauce

4 white cabbage leaves,
  shredded

4 hard-boiled eggs, cooled,
  peeled and halved

4 tablespoons Fried Red-skin
  Peanuts (page 240)

4 teaspoons Crispy Fried Onions
  (page 238) or shop-bought
  fried onions

To serve

4 garlic cloves, peeled

2 limes, cut into wedges

Chilli Oil (page 236)

point, add a little more water and continue stirring every now and then. Now add a ladleful of the chicken broth to the sauce and stir well before adding the chicken meat. Set the chicken sauce to one side but keep warm.

For the turmeric oil, put the turmeric in a heatproof bowl. Heat the oil in a frying pan over a high heat for a couple of minutes, until sizzling, then pour on to the turmeric. Allow to settle before whisking. Set to one side.

Heat 2 tablespoons of oil in the same pan over a medium heat. Add the fishcake and fry for 5 minutes until cooked. Set to one side.

When you're ready to serve, thoroughly drain the shaved shallots.

Reheat the noodles by placing the colander in your sink and pouring a full kettle of boiling water over them. Divide the noodles between four pasta dishes. To each dish, add 1 tablespoon of toasted gram flour, 3 tablespoons of chicken sauce, 1 tablespoon of turmeric oil and 1 tablespoon of fish sauce. Now add a few slices of fishcake, some shaved shallots, shredded cabbage and an egg. Lastly, garnish each dish with a tablespoon of fried red-skin peanuts, a teaspoon of crispy fried onions and some chopped coriander, a garlic clove and a wedge of lime.

Bring the broth back to a simmer, then pour into four Chinese/small soup bowls. Add some chopped coriander and freshly ground black pepper to each bowl. Serve the noodles immediately and encourage your diners to get stuck in and use their hands to mix and eat the noodles, though cutlery is allowed! Arrange the bowls of broth on the side with Chinese spoons and hand out chilli oil and extra lime wedges for people to help themselves. This dish can be eaten warm or at room temperature.

Mandalay Pork & Round Rice Noodles

MANDALAY MEESHAY   မန္တလေးမြီးရေ

I think this is the Burmese dish that I love best, because it has always been served at family parties and was the first dish that I learned how to make. It's also an example of the best of Mandalay's street food. My grandfather's favourite pastime was accosting passing snack-sellers, and I had him on red alert for the *Mandalay meeshay* seller who'd trot past with his wares hanging off a pole balanced on his shoulder. The pork sauce is the same used with *Mogok meeshay* (and I believe *meeshay* is in turn a corruption of the Chinese *mǐxiàn*, which is more or less the same noodle). However, there's an equally popular version of *Mandalay meeshay* that you'll find in restaurants and homes made with chicken sauce – just use the same sauce as in the recipe for Mandalay Chicken Noodle Salad (page 117) but omit the ground turmeric.

Serves 4-6

400g dried thick, round rice
   noodles (Vietnamese bún or
   Guilin rice vermicelli)

For the broth
1 x 1kg piece pork belly
½ teaspoon MSG or 1 tablespoon
   chicken or vegetable bouillon
1 tablespoon caster sugar
½ teaspoon salt

For the crispy omelette
1 heaped tablespoon
   self-raising flour
2 eggs
½ teaspoon salt
8 tablespoons groundnut oil

For the coriander and garlic salsa
8 garlic cloves, peeled
½ teaspoon salt
large handful of coriander leaves

For the condiments
Rice Sauce (page 243)
Chinese black vinegar
yellow soybean sauce
light soy sauce
freshly ground black pepper

... continued on page 120

Put the noodles in a heatproof bowl. Pour enough just-boiled water over to submerge and leave to soak for 1 hour. Drain the noodles and then re-submerge with just-boiled water and soak for another 10 minutes. Drain in a colander and rinse thoroughly under cold running water, then set to one side in the colander so that the noodles can continue to drain.

Now make the broth. Put the pork belly, MSG, sugar and salt in a saucepan with 1 litre of water. Bring to the boil, then reduce the heat to medium-low and simmer for 3 hours, skimming any scum from the surface. Transfer the pork to a small saucepan and use kitchen scissors to snip it into small chunks. Add 2 ladlefuls of the pork broth to moisten and stir this pork sauce, then set to one side. Keep the broth and the pork sauce warm.

Make the crispy omelette next. Combine the flour, eggs, salt and 2 tablespoons of cold water in a bowl and whisk to a smooth batter. Pour the oil into a wok or large frying pan and place over a high heat. When you can feel waves of heat rising from the oil with the palm of your hand, swirl the oil around, then pour the batter evenly into the wok or pan; the batter will puff up almost immediately to form a large cloud. Leave for 30 seconds before using a spatula to 'chop' the cloud into big fluffy pieces. After 1 minute, flip each piece gently to ensure an even colour on both sides. When the omelette pieces are crisp and golden brown, scoop out with a slotted spoon and drain on kitchen paper. Pour the oil you've used for frying (known in Burmese as '*si chet*', which literally means 'cooked oil' – see also page 239) into a small bowl and reserve for dressing the noodles later.

For the coriander and garlic salsa, pound the garlic using a mortar and pestle (or blitz in a food processor), until you have a rough paste. Scoop into a small

...continued on page 120

For the garnish
Shan Mustard Green Pickle
    (page 194) or Water Pickle
    (page 243)
beansprouts, tails removed and
    discarded, blanched
Crispy Fried Onions (page 238) or
    shop-bought fried onions
Chilli Oil (page 236), to taste

bowl and add the salt and 50ml of water and mix well. Next add the chopped coriander leaves and stir in gently.

When you're ready to serve, bring the broth back to a vigorous simmer and keep hot. Reheat the noodles by placing the colander in your sink and pouring a kettleful of boiling water over them. Divide the noodles between four bowls. To each bowl, add 2 tablespoons of rice sauce, 3 tablespoons of pork sauce and 1 tablespoon of 'cooked' oil. Now add 1 tablespoon of black vinegar, 1 teaspoon of yellow soybean sauce and 1 teaspoon of light soy sauce. Lastly add 2 tablespoons of pickle, 1 tablespoon of coriander and garlic salsa, 1 teaspoon of crispy fried onions and 1 tablespoon of beansprouts.

Pour the broth into four Chinese/small soup bowls. Add 1 teaspoon of coriander and garlic salsa, ¼ teaspoon of yellow soybean sauce and some freshly ground black pepper to each bowl.

Serve the noodles immediately, with chopsticks and metal Chinese/Thai spoons. Arrange the bowls of pork broth on the side and some chilli oil for people to help themselves.

Mogok Pork & Round Rice Noodles

MOGOK MEESHAY　　　　မိုးကုတ်မြီးရှေ

This Mogok dish of rice noodles and pork is an absolute favourite of mine. It's easy to make, so I do so at least once a week, and I also request it from my mother when I visit. Whenever we arrive at my aunt's house in Yangon after a long and tiring flight, this is the dish that I dive into first, amongst the many she has ready waiting for us. It's sweet, sour, and garlicky, restorative yet packed full of flavour, and it makes me feel like I've come home.

Serves 4

400g dried thick, round rice
　noodles (Vietnamese bún or
　Guilin rice vermicelli)
freshly ground black pepper

For the broth
1 x 1kg piece pork belly
½ teaspoon MSG or 1 tablespoon
　chicken or vegetable bouillon
1 tablespoon caster sugar
½ teaspoon salt

For the condiments
Rice Sauce (page 243)
2 tablespoons tamarind paste
1 teaspoon sugar
50ml malt vinegar
1 teaspoon salt
¼ bunch of coriander
4 tablespoons light soy sauce
4 teaspoons dark soy sauce

For the garnish
'Cooked' Oil (page 239)
Crispy Fried Onions (page 238) or
　shop-bought fried onions
Crispy Fried Garlic (page 238) or
　shop-bought fried garlic
Chilli Oil (page 236)

Put the noodles in a heatproof bowl, submerge with just-boiled water and leave to soak for 1 hour. Drain the noodles and then re-submerge with just-boiled water and soak for another 10 minutes. Drain in a colander and rinse thoroughly with running cold water, then set to one side in the colander so that any residual water can continue to drain.

Now make the broth. Put the pork belly, MSG, sugar and salt in a saucepan with 1 litre of water. Bring to the boil, then reduce the heat to medium-low and simmer for 3 hours, skimming any scum from the surface. Transfer the pork to a small saucepan and use kitchen scissors to snip it into small chunks. Add 2 ladlefuls of the pork broth to moisten and stir this pork sauce, then set to one side. Keep the broth and the pork sauce warm.

Make the rice sauce (see page 243), then add the tamarind paste, sugar, vinegar and salt and mix thoroughly. Simmer for 10 minutes over a medium-low heat and set to one side.

Use a mortar and pestle to grind the coriander stems to a paste (or finely chop by hand). Roughly chop the coriander leaves. Put the coriander stem paste in a small bowl and add 50ml of water and a pinch of salt. Mix well, then add the coriander leaves and stir gently.

When you're ready to serve, reheat the noodles by placing the colander in your sink and pouring a kettleful of just-boiled water over them. Divide the noodles between four noodle bowls. To each bowl, add 3 tablespoons of tamarind rice sauce, 3 tablespoons of pork sauce and 2 ladles full of pork broth. Now add 1 tablespoon of light soy sauce and 1 teaspoon of dark soy sauce to each bowl. Lastly add 1 tablespoon of 'cooked' oil and 1 tablespoon of coriander salsa to each bowl, and sprinkle some crispy fried onions and garlic on top.

Heat the remaining broth until simmering, then divide between four Chinese/small soup bowls and add 1 teaspoon of coriander salsa and some freshly ground black pepper to each bowl. Serve the noodles immediately, with chopsticks and metal Chinese/Thai spoons. Arrange the bowls of pork broth on the side and some chilli oil for people to help themselves.

Meat

A-THAR-ZONE

အသားစုံ

Seeing as Burma is a predominantly Buddhist country and I myself was raised as a Theravadin Buddhist, I am often asked how it is that I happen to eat meat. The Buddhist precepts say you must not take a life, but they do not actually say that you cannot eat meat. In fact, the Buddha himself ate meat, as do Burmese Buddhist monks (I'm slightly ashamed to say I've even been jealous, as they are always offered the choicest cuts in their alms). This may sound very much like shifty semantics, but all I can do is hold up my hands and say that Buddhism is meant to be about taking the Middle Way i.e. everything in moderation.

In fact, the Burmese do not tend to eat a huge amount of meat anyway. The portion of meat described as 'the size of a pack of playing cards' that is so often recommended in Western diets would actually be overkill to the average Burmese person. In terms of plate percentages, 70 per cent would be the rice or noodles, 20 per cent vegetables or salad and only 10 per cent would be meat.

But a little goes a very long way, especially when it's a rich, spiced curry, a vegetable-heavy stir-fry or a lush, gravied stew.

Classic Pork Curry

WET THAR HNAT ဝက်သားနှပ်

This classic curry from Mogok, my mother's home town, is more or less used to wean Burmese children – my nephews and nieces can eat bowls and bowls of the stuff, as it's sweet and mild, yet addictive.

Before my youngest nephew could talk properly, whenever he visited his grandparents, he'd ask for 'pok and yice' (pork and rice), and I'm pleased to say that my own children are now equally big fans.

Serves 4-6

1kg pork leg or shoulder,
  with some fat, diced into
  2.5cm cubes
100ml malt vinegar
4 medium onions, peeled
2cm piece of ginger, peeled
4 tablespoons groundnut oil or
  other neutral-tasting oil
1 tablespoon sugar
1 tablespoon light soy sauce
1 tablespoon dark soy sauce
1 teaspoon freshly ground
  black pepper

Toss the pork thoroughly in the vinegar and then discard the vinegar. (This imparts a slight sourness and is traditionally thought to clean the pork.) Place the pork in a large saucepan and add enough water to just submerge. Cover the pan with a lid and bring to the boil over a high heat. Turn the heat down to medium-low and continue to simmer, with the lid on, for 15 minutes.

Remove the pork and set to one side; pour the pork juices into a bowl and reserve. Do not wash the saucepan – you'll reuse it later.

Slice the onions into wedges. Pound the ginger into a rough pulp using a pestle and mortar. Add 2 tablespoons of water in the well of the mortar and stir to make ginger juice. You can also blitz the ginger with the water in a food processor but all you want is the juice, so you'll need to strain it. Whichever method you choose, make sure to squeeze the pulp to get all the juices out and discard said pulp.

Heat the oil in the saucepan over a medium-high heat. Add the pork cubes and toss for 4–5 minutes until browned all over. Add the onion wedges and ginger juice and stir-fry for another minute. Add the reserved pork juices, sugar, light and dark soy sauces and pepper, along with 500ml of water. Cover the pan with a lid and bring to the boil.

Now turn down the heat to medium-low and simmer for 1½ hours until the sauce is sticky and reduced.

When the time is up, the pork should be tender and fall apart if you poke it with a fork. Serve with lots of fluffy white rice and stir-fried greens on the side.

Cook's Note

After you've added all the ingredients and brought them to the boil, you could transfer everything to a lidded casserole dish and place in an oven preheated to 160°C/140°C Fan/Gas Mark 3 for 1½ hours. This will give the same tender pork, but the sauce will be much thinner and there will be more of it.

This curry freezes very well and will keep frozen for up to a month.

Pork & Green Mango Curry

WET THAR THAYET CHIN   ဝက်သားသရက်ချဉ်

Although we Burmese adore mangoes so much that they appear in our proverbs, oddly enough they don't feature in our desserts. We'll happily gorge on the fresh, ripe fruit whenever, but whilst green, we keep them savoury – we like to eat them dipped in sambals or in salads and here we even serve them up in a curry. Make the mango pickle the night before – it also works well as a chutney in sandwiches and on the side with roast meats.

Serves 4-6

For the pickled mango
2 small green (unripe) mangoes
2 tablespoons salt
1 teaspoon sugar
juice of 1 lemon

For the pork curry
1kg pork belly, cut into
    2.5cm dice
100ml malt vinegar
1 medium onion, peeled and
    roughly chopped
2 spring onions, green and
    white parts
2cm piece of ginger, peeled
2 garlic cloves, peeled
1 medium tomato, roughly
    chopped
1 green finger chilli
3 sprigs of coriander, stems
    and leaves
90ml groundnut oil or other
    neutral-tasting oil
1 teaspoon ground turmeric
1 teaspoon paprika
1 tablespoon shrimp paste
    (*belacan*)
½ teaspoon mild chilli powder
¼ teaspoon MSG or ½
    tablespoon chicken or
    vegetable bouillon

The night before making this dish, make the pickled mango. Remove the stone from the mango and shred the flesh, including the peel, as thinly as possible using a mandoline or knife. Place in a small saucepan and pour boiling water over to blanch the mango. Now drain the mango and place in a bowl. Add the salt, sugar and lemon juice, and mix well. Leave overnight to pickle lightly.

In a bowl, toss the pork belly thoroughly in the vinegar and then drain. Place the pork belly in a large saucepan and add enough water to just submerge the pork. Cover the pan with a lid and bring to the boil over a high heat. Turn the heat down to medium-low and simmer the pork, covered, for 15 minutes.

Remove the pork and set to one side; pour the pork juices into a bowl and reserve. Do not rinse out the pan – you'll reuse it later.

Blitz the onion, spring onions, ginger, garlic, tomato, green chilli and coriander with 2 tablespoons of water in a food processor or blender to a rough paste.

Heat the oil over a medium-high heat in the pan used for the pork. Add the turmeric and paprika to the oil and allow to sizzle for a few seconds. Add the onion paste and fry for 5 minutes, until fragrant. Add the pork, shrimp paste, chilli powder, MSG, reserved pork juices and 200ml of water. Cover the pan with the lid and bring to the boil.

Now turn the heat down to medium-low and simmer for 1 hour. Drain the pickled mango, squeeze dry, and add to the pan. Stir well and simmer for another 10 minutes.

When the time is up, the pork should be tender and fall apart if you poke it with a fork. Served with steamed rice and crispy shrimp relish (page 212).

Pork Belly & Bamboo Shoot Stew

WET THAR HMYIT CHIN ဝက်သားမျှစ်ချဉ်

This lovely, piquant stew is made with tender bamboo shoot tips rather than the slightly bland and woody strips that most people are familiar with. When you cut the tips in half, it exposes the delicate ribs within that are remarkably pretty. This stew is one of the few dishes where I'd eat my rice with a spoon; I adore pouring the broth on top until the rice is almost swimming (a practice known as *yay baw-law*). The stew goes very well with Crispy Shrimp Relish (page 212), which I sprinkle all over before digging in.

Serves 4-6

10 tablespoons groundnut oil or other neutral-tasting oil

1kg boneless pork belly, cut into 5cm cubes

400g bamboo shoot tips (see Cook's Note), halved

For the base

1 onion, peeled and roughly chopped

2 spring onions, green and white parts

stems from ½ bunch coriander

4 garlic cloves, peeled

1 finger chilli

For the seasoning

2 tablespoons tomato purée or juice only from a 400g tin plum tomatoes

1 tablespoon rice flour

1 tablespoon shrimp paste (*belacan*)

1 teaspoon salt

¼ teaspoon MSG or ½ tablespoon chicken or vegetable bouillon

juice of ¼ lemon

Combine all the base ingredients in a blender or food processor and blitz to a fine paste. Set to one side.

Heat 6 tablespoons of the oil in a stockpot or deep saucepan over a medium-high heat. Add the pork belly and toss for 10 minutes, until browned all over. Remove the pork belly and set to one side. Do not wash out the stockpot.

Heat the remaining 4 tablespoons of oil over a medium-high heat in the stockpot. Add the paste and fry for 3–4 minutes, until fragrant.

Now add the seasonings, and stir-fry for 2–3 minutes. Tip the pork belly cubes back into the stockpot, stir to coat the pork in the paste and fry for another 2–3 minutes. Pour over 1 litre of water, add the bamboo shoots and then bring to the boil. Immediately turn down the heat to medium and simmer for 1 hour. Serve with steamed rice, crispy shrimp relish (page 212) and *balachaung* (page 211).

Cook's Note

Bamboo shoot tips are available at all Asian supermarkets and usually come in tins or packets. At a pinch, you could substitute tinned bamboo shoot slices but they won't be as tender as the bamboo tips.

Pork with Pickled Mustard Greens

WET THAR MON-NYIN CHIN   ဝက်သားမုန်ညင်းချဉ်

There are actually two versions of this pork and mustard green dish, both of which come from Mogok. The first is basically made when you have leftover Classic Pork Curry (page 126) – shredded mustard greens are added to the curry and it's cooked down until the sauce has darkened, is almost completely reduced and the meat is falling apart. I prefer this version, which is made from scratch and is sweeter, lighter and fresher tasting.

Serves 4

350g sweet preserved mustard
  greens in brine
1 x 500g piece of medium-fatty
  pork belly
2 tablespoons sugar
1 teaspoon salt
4 tablespoons groundnut oil
  or other neutral-tasting oil
3 garlic cloves, peeled and sliced
1cm slice of ginger, cut into fine
  matchsticks
2 spring onions, both white and
  green parts, cut into
  fine matchsticks
1 tomato, diced
2 tablespoons light soy sauce
1 tablespoon dark soy sauce
2 finger chillies, cut into fine
  matchsticks (optional)

Shred the preserved mustard greens and do not throw away the brine.

Place the pork belly, sugar and salt in a saucepan with 500ml of water and bring to the boil over a high heat. Turn the heat down to medium-low and poach for 15 minutes. Remove the pork using a pair of tongs, reserving the stock. Slice the pork into nugget-sized chunks.

Heat the oil in a wok or large frying pan over a medium-high heat. Fry the pork for 4 minutes and then add the garlic, ginger and spring onions, and fry for another 3 minutes until fragrant.

Now add the tomato, shredded mustard greens and its brine, soy sauces, the chilli if using and the reserved stock. Toss everything together, turn the heat down to medium and simmer for 20 minutes or until the sauce is reduced to the consistency of runny honey. Serve with plenty of steamed rice and the shrimp and cabbage soup (page 87) on the side.

Braised Beef Curry

AMÈ HNAT   အမဲနှပ်

Amè hnat is the dish that we like to serve at family gatherings, as it's so rich that it can be the star with lots of different side dishes. It reminds me of the Malaysian dish beef *rendang* but has more sauce. You can add a couple of quartered boiled potatoes to the curry near the end of the cooking time, which will soak up all the lovely juices – my eldest niece likes to fish these 'gravied potatoes' out for herself and I think she likes them more than the beef!

Serves 6

8 tablespoons groundnut oil or
    other neutral-tasting oil
1kg beef, cut into 5cm cubes

For the base
3 onions, roughly chopped
1 spring onion, roughly chopped
2 tomatoes, roughly chopped
5cm piece of ginger
5 garlic cloves
bunch of coriander, stems only
1 green finger chilli
6 curry leaves

For seasoning
1 teaspoon ground turmeric
1 teaspoon salt
¼ teaspoon MSG or ½
    tablespoon chicken or
    vegetable bouillon
2 teaspoons paprika
1 tablespoon ground coriander

Heat 4 tablespoons of the oil in a large saucepan over a medium-high heat and add the beef. Fry for 20 minutes, turning the cubes from time to time so they don't stick to the pan. Juices will seep out but these will reduce down and the meat will brown.

Meanwhile, add the base ingredients along with 1 tablespoon of water to a blender or food processor. Blitz to a rough paste.

Transfer the meat from the pan to a dish and set aside. Add the remaining 4 tablespoons of oil to the pan used to brown the beef. Heat over a medium-high heat and add the onion-tomato paste. Add the seasonings, stir and then fry for 5 minutes until fragrant. Add the beef and 1.5 litres of water and cover the pan with a lid. Turn the heat down to medium-low and cook for 2½ hours until the beef is tender and falling apart, stirring occasionally to stop the curry from sticking to the base of the pan.

When it's ready, serve the curry with steamed rice, any of the soups and a vegetable dish or salad to balance the richness. It also goes well with Indian breads, such as naan, puri and paratha.

Lime Leaf Pot Roast Beef

AMÈ THAR PYOTE KYAW   အမဲသားပြုတ်ကြော်

This popular beef dish is often eaten for brunch with plain rice or Golden
Sticky Rice (page 97). The beef itself is dry almost to the point of jerky, so if
you don't scarf it all at once, it keeps for a couple of days in the fridge.

Serves 4–6

800g braising beef, cut into
  2cm dice
50ml vinegar
5cm piece of ginger, peeled
6 garlic cloves, peeled
100ml groundnut oil or other
  neutral-tasting oil, plus
  2 tablespoons
1 teaspoon ground turmeric
4 lime leaves or 1 teaspoon
  lime leaf powder
1½ tablespoons fish sauce
1 teaspoon sugar
1 teaspoon ground white pepper
1 teaspoon dark soy sauce
4 dried red finger chillies
  (optional)
Crispy Fried Garlic (page 238)
  (optional)

In a large bowl, toss the beef in the vinegar and set to one side for 15 minutes.

Blitz the ginger with 4 tablespoons of water in a small food processor
or blender. Take out two-thirds of the pulp and squeeze it, returning any
juices back into the food processor bowl. Discard the pulp, or use it for
other purposes.

Add the garlic to the food processor and blitz to as smooth a paste as possible.

Heat the oil in a wok or large frying pan (with a lid) over a high heat. Add the
turmeric to the oil and allow to sizzle for a few seconds. Drain the beef, toss
through the turmeric oil and fry for 10 minutes. A lot of liquid will come out of
the beef, but it will reduce down to nothing by the end of the cooking time
and the beef will start to sear and brown.

Now add the ginger-garlic paste from the blender to the wok but do not wash
out the food processor bowl/blender jug. Toss the beef through the paste and
fry over a high heat for 2–3 minutes.

Swirl 250ml of water in the food processor/blender jug and then pour this
to the wok. Add the lime leaves, fish sauce, sugar and white pepper, and toss
everything through again. Turn the heat down to medium-low and cover with
a lid. Simmer for 30 minutes, until the beef is tender and the sauce has
reduced slightly.

Add the dark soy sauce and dried chillies and turn the heat up to high. Stir-fry
for another 5 minutes, until the beef and chillies become dark and glossy.
Scatter with the crispy fried garlic, if using, and serve with steamed rice and
bean soup (page 91).

Goat & Split Pea Curry

SEIK THAR KALAPE HIN   ဆိတ်သားကုလားပဲဟင်း

This curry is similar to the Indian dish lamb *dhansak*, but made with split peas, which the Burmese prefer to lentils, and goat meat, as lamb is scarcer in Burma.

With its Indian influences, unsurprisingly it goes very well with *paratha* and *poori* as well as Buttered Lentil Rice (page 94).

Serves 4–6

200g dried yellow split peas
120ml groundnut oil or other
  neutral-tasting oil
1 teaspoon ground turmeric
1kg goat meat, diced
2 teaspoons ground coriander
1 teaspoon ground cumin
1 teaspoon paprika
½ teaspoon mild chilli powder
¼ teaspoon MSG or ½
  tablespoon chicken or
  vegetable bouillon
1 tablespoon fish sauce

For the curry paste
1 onion, quartered
2 spring onions
1 tomato, quartered
6 curry leaves
1 finger chilli
2cm piece of ginger
2 garlic cloves
4 sprigs of coriander

Soak the split peas overnight in a bowl of cold water.

Blitz the curry paste ingredients to a rough paste in a food processor or blender and set to one side.

Heat the oil in a large saucepan over a high heat. Add the turmeric to the oil, remove from the hob, and let it sizzle for a few seconds. Return to the hob over a medium-high heat. Add the curry paste (do not wash out the food processor bowl/blender jug) and fry the paste for 5 minutes, until fragrant.

Add the meat, spices and MSG, and fry for another 5 minutes. Drain the split peas, add them to the pan and fry for another 5 minutes.

Swirl 400ml of water in the food processor bowl/blender jug to sweep up any leftover paste and pour this water into the pan. Add the fish sauce and bring to the boil. Cover the pan with a lid, reduce the heat to medium-low and simmer for 2 hours, until the sauce reduces by a third and the meat is tender and falls apart when prodded with a fork.

Serve with plain or buttered lentil rice (page 94).

Cook's Note
You can replace goat meat with the same quantity of lamb neck or shoulder as goat meat can be hard to come by unless you have a Caribbean shop nearby.

Meatball Curry

ATHAR-LONE HIN အသားလုံးဟင်း

Meatball curry is popular throughout Burma, but especially in the Upper region. It is usually made with goat (*seik-thar*), but beef (*amè-thar*) is also common. Lamb makes an excellent substitute, although is rarely used in Burma, partly because the Burmese word for 'lamb' is *thoh*, which also sounds like our word for 'rotten'.

The curry also works well made using 50:50 pork and beef mince, and the higher up you travel in Burma, the more likely pork will feature in the mix.

Serves 4–6

For the sauce
180ml groundnut oil or other neutral-tasting oil
4 onions, diced
1 spring onion, finely chopped
5 garlic cloves, chopped
1 teaspoon ground turmeric
400g tin chopped tomatoes
3 red finger chillies (optional)
1 tablespoon paprika
2 tablespoons fish sauce

For the meatballs (makes 20–25)
500g minced goat (substitute beef or lamb) or 50:50 with minced pork
1 onion or 2 spring onions, finely chopped
1 bunch of coriander, stems finely chopped, leaves torn and reserved to garnish
4 tablespoons ground arrowroot or tapioca starch
2 egg whites
1 teaspoon salt
¼ teaspoon MSG or ½ tablespoon chicken or vegetable bouillon

Heat the oil in a saucepan over a medium heat. Add the onions, spring onions, garlic and turmeric and fry for 5 minutes, until soft. Add the tomatoes but don't throw away the tin. Fry for another 10 minutes and then add two tins full of water. Turn the heat to high, bring to the boil and then turn the heat to medium-low, add the chillies, paprika and fish sauce and simmer for 45 minutes.

Meanwhile, mix all the meatball ingredients in a large bowl with 2 tablespoons of water and then form into ping-pong-sized balls – you'll make about 25.

Add enough water to a large frying pan to come up to 2cm in depth. Bring to the boil, add the meatballs in one layer and then turn the heat down to medium. Leave to cook for about 5 minutes or until the meatballs are firm.

Continue to cook the meatballs until the water sizzles away, the meatballs begin to brown (flip again to brown all over) and the fat begins to seep out of the meatballs – this method is called *see-pyan* in Burmese, meaning 'the oil returns'. Use a slotted spoon to transfer the meatballs to the tomato sauce.

Heat through so the flavours of the sauce and the meatballs mingle and everything is piping hot and then serve, scattered with fresh coriander leaves.

Cook's Note
Traditionally, this dish is served with steamed rice but you could also eat it with naan bread, or even serve on noodles for a Burmese take on spaghetti and meatballs.

Chicken & Eggs

KYET THAR, KYET U, BE U

ကြက်သား, ကြက်ဥ, ဘဲဥ

Chicken in Burma is generally eaten on the bone, because the old saying that 'the nearer the bone, the sweeter the meat' is completely true. Eggs are a particular favourite as they can be employed in Burmese soups, stir-fries, salads and even curries. Duck eggs (*be u*) are more common than hen's eggs (*kyet u*) in Burma, since more ducks are kept than chickens, and this happy situation means that the sunniest yolks end up in the pot.

Classic Chicken Curry

KYET THAR SEE-PYAN

This is the archetypal Burmese chicken curry – *see-pyan* means 'the oil returns' and refers to a special technique of simmering the sauce. Being relatively mild, this curry is usually eaten with lots of side dishes, and goes particularly well as part of a spread with *Balachaung* (page 211) or Pounded Fish Paste Relish (page 207), Classic Sour Soup (page 88), Braised Butter Beans (page 184), Roselle Leaves with Bamboo Shoots (page 180) and of course rice.

Serves 4-6

120ml groundnut oil or other
   neutral-tasting oil
1 teaspoon ground turmeric
1 tablespoon paprika
1 teaspoon shrimp paste
   (*belacan*)
¼ teaspoon MSG or ½
   tablespoon chicken bouillon
1 tablespoon fish sauce
500g chicken thighs, skinned
500g chicken drumsticks,
   skinned

For the curry paste

2 onions, quartered
1 tomato, quartered
2 spring onions, green and
   white parts
4 garlic cloves
2cm piece of ginger
handful of coriander stems

Blitz the curry paste ingredients to a rough paste in a food processor or blender and set to one side.

Heat the oil in a large saucepan over a high heat. Add the turmeric to the oil, remove from the hob, and let sizzle for a few seconds. Return the pan to the hob and reduce the heat to medium-high. Add the curry paste (do not wash out the food processor bowl or blender jug) and fry the paste for 5 minutes, until fragrant.

Swirl 200ml of water in the food processor bowl (or blender jug) to sweep up any paste left inside and tip into the saucepan. Turn the heat to high and add the paprika, shrimp paste, MSG and fish sauce. Bring to the boil, stir thoroughly and cook for another 5 minutes until the sauce darkens and the oil separates from the rest of the sauce and rises as a ring of oil around the inner edges of the pan (this is known as *see-pyan* or 'the oil returns').

Now add the chicken pieces. Turn the heat to medium-low, place a lid on the pan and simmer for 30 minutes. Serve with plain or buttered lentil rice (page 94) and a vegetable dish or salad.

BFC – Burmese Fried Chicken

KYET THAR KYAW   

I associate Burmese fried chicken with road trips, as when we're travelling around Burma and make a pit stop in any village, it seems that women always come rushing to our rolled-down windows to sell us baskets of their freshly fried chicken (I call them The Chicken Ladies).

    I'd say BFC is better than KFC and it definitely has far fewer ingredients. It's commonly eaten with a plate of hot rice that's been drizzled with some of the oil used for frying (*si chet* – see also page 239) and sprinkled with a little salt. BFC is also great eaten cold … if you can manage to wait that long. Make it once and you're addicted for life.

Serves 4

750g small chicken thighs or
   drumsticks or wings, skin on
juice of ½ lime
groundnut oil or other neutral-
   tasting oil, for frying
Chilli Sauce (page 236), to serve

For the dry rub
2 tablespoons self-raising flour
1 tablespoon ground turmeric
1 teaspoon garlic powder
1 teaspoon ground ginger
1 teaspoon salt
1 teaspoon ground white pepper
½ teaspoon MSG or 1 tablespoon
   chicken or vegetable bouillon

Place the chicken pieces in a large bowl and squeeze over the lime juice. Use clean hands to lightly massage the lime juice into the chicken, pour away any excess and set to one side.

Thoroughly mix the dry rub ingredients in another large bowl and then coat the chicken pieces evenly with the mix. Leave to marinate for 2 hours.

Heat a 8cm depth of oil in a wok or large frying pan to 175°C (or use a deep-fat fryer). Gently lower 2–3 chicken pieces, skin-side down, into the hot oil, being careful not to crowd the pan. The oil should sizzle and bubble gently around each piece of chicken. Fry for 6–8 minutes, or until crispy and golden on one side, flip and continue to fry until the other side is just as golden.

Drain one piece of chicken and poke with a skewer to check that the juices run clear – if so, drain all the crispy chicken on kitchen paper. Continue to fry the remaining chicken pieces in batches.

Eat immediately with chilli sauce (page 236).

Burmese Masala Chicken

KYET THAR MASALA HIN ကြက်သားမဆလာဟင်း

This is the Burmese take on a classic Indian curry, and as a result, it's served just as often with Indian breads such as *poori* as it is with rice (though it's brilliant with Buttered Lentil Rice – page 94). There's not a lot more to say about it, except Rukmini, the lovely food stylist who worked on this book, declared it was the best chicken curry she had ever eaten (cue shameless gloating from me).

Serves 4–6

90ml groundnut oil or other
  neutral-tasting oil
1 teaspoon ground turmeric
2 potatoes, peeled and quartered
8 chicken thigh fillets
  (about 750g)
¼ teaspoon MSG or ½
  tablespoon chicken or
  vegetable bouillon
½ teaspoon salt

For the curry paste
2 onions, quartered
6 curry leaves
2 finger chillies
2 garlic cloves, peeled
2cm piece of ginger
3 sprigs of coriander
1 tablespoon ground cumin
1 teaspoon paprika
1 teaspoon ground coriander
½ teaspoon mild chilli powder

Blitz the curry paste ingredients in a food processor or blender to form a thick paste and set to one side.

Heat the oil on a medium-high heat in a large saucepan and add the turmeric. Remove from the hob, let it sizzle for a few seconds and then return to the hob and add the curry paste (do not wash out the food processor bowl or blender jug). Fry the paste for 5 minutes until fragrant.

Swirl 100ml of water in the food processor bowl or blender jug to sweep up any paste and add to the pan. Add the potatoes, MSG and salt, cover the pan with a lid, and continue to simmer over a medium-high heat for 15 minutes.

Add the chicken, cover with the lid, reduce the heat to medium-low and simmer for 20 minutes or until the sauce is reduced. Serve with plain or buttered lentil rice (page 94).

Bachelor's Chicken Curry

KYET THAR KARLA-THAR HIN ‎ကြက်သားကာလသားဟင်း

The full moon of November heralds *Tazaungdaing* in Burma, a festival of mischief-making where young men are encouraged to go on a kind of scavenger hunt. In villages, they 'steal' chickens, which have been deliberately left in the backyards of rich people to create a midnight feast – in towns, they're more likely to just buy the bird. This is the hearty festival dish they make – it's easy and you use the bones and all. *Karla-thar* means 'sons of our times' and *hin* means a sauced dish and is usually translated as curry, though this is more of a stew. Eat this curry with Charred Tomato Salsa (page 216) for a match made in heaven.

Serves 8

2 large onions, roughly chopped

2 spring onions, green and white parts roughly chopped

4 large ripe tomatoes or 400g tin plum tomatoes

2 garlic heads, separated into cloves and peeled

8cm piece of ginger, peeled and roughly chopped

stems from a small bunch of coriander

4 bird's eye chillies

4 tablespoons fish sauce

2 tablespoons sugar

2 tablespoons shrimp paste (*belacan*)

1 tablespoon mild chilli powder

1 tablespoon paprika

4 tablespoons groundnut oil or other neutral-tasting oil

1 cockerel or large chicken, jointed (about 1.5kg)

500g bottle gourd or winter melon or daikon or 4 courgettes, peeled and cut into chunks

Place all the ingredients in a food processor or blender, except for the oil, bird and the gourd, and blitz into a rough paste.

Heat the oil in a deep saucepan or stockpot over a medium heat and fry the paste until fragrant, at least 5 minutes. Add the chicken and continue to fry until browned a little.

Pour in enough water to submerge the chicken, bring to the boil over a high heat, then turn down to low and simmer, covered, for 4 hours for cockerel or 2 hours for a large chicken. Top up with extra water whenever the chicken rises above the level.

Half an hour before you intend to dish up, chuck in the pieces of gourd and allow them to cook through.

Serve with steamed rice and charred tomato salsa (page 216). This is a broth-like dish, and your rice should be swimming in rich gravy.

Cook's Note

A slow cooker works particularly well for making this dish – after frying the chicken and paste together, transfer it all to a slow cooker, add enough water to cover and then set it and forget about it.

Fragrant Cinnamon Chicken

KYET THAR HIN-HMWE   ကြက်သားဟင်းမွှေး

There's a certain coffee shop that is filled with the scent of cinnamon and whenever I go by, I'm suddenly ravenous. I finally made the connection that it reminded me of this dish, *kyet thar hin-hmwe* – literally 'fragrant chicken curry'. I cooked it at my very first pop-up, which was held at the Wild Garlic, the restaurant by Mat Follas who won MasterChef in 2009. One of the guests was a cattle farmer who declared he would give up beef for this recipe!

Serves 4-6

4 tablespoons groundnut oil
  or other neutral-tasting oil
6 onions, diced
½ teaspoon ground turmeric
1 tablespoon sugar
1 tablespoon dark soy sauce
1 tablespoon garlic powder
1 tablespoon ground ginger
1 tablespoon ground cinnamon
  or 4 cinnamon sticks
½ teaspoon mild chilli powder
½ teaspoon paprika
½ teaspoon freshly ground
  black pepper
¼ teaspoon MSG or ½
  tablespoon chicken bouillon
8 chicken thigh fillets
  (about 750g)

Heat the oil in a large saucepan over a high heat and add the onions and turmeric. Fry for 2–3 minutes, then turn down to medium-high and fry for another 10 minutes until fragrant and the onions translucent. Add 200ml of water and all the remaining ingredients except for the chicken, and then simmer for 15 minutes.

Now add the chicken and stir so the chicken is coated with the sauce, then cover with a lid and simmer again for 30 minutes. Serve with steamed rice.

Burmese Chicken Nuggets

KYET SA-OOT KYAW

When I was little, my mother gave this recipe to a friend of hers who pestered her for it for ages, and said friend promptly tried to pass it off as her own creation. Let's just say they don't talk any more. My own kids call these 'chewy chicken' as they're more tender than standard chicken nuggets, and they frequently clamour for 'chewy chicken and rice'.

A pork version called *wet sa-oot kyaw* is also very popular in Burma, especially Mogok (of course). To make this, use two fat slices of pork belly cut into strips instead of the chicken and proceed as per the recipe.

Serves 4-6

2 medium chicken breasts
   or thighs, sliced into
   5cm x 1cm strips
groundnut oil or other neutral-
   tasting oil, for frying
Chilli Sauce (page 236), to serve

For the batter
2 tablespoons self-raising flour
2 tablespoons rice flour
2 tablespoons glutinous rice flour
2 tablespoons ground arrowroot
2 egg whites
¼ teaspoon salt
¼ teaspoon ground white pepper
¼ teaspoon MSG or ½
   tablespoon chicken or
   vegetable bouillon

Mix all the batter ingredients in a large bowl and add 1–2 tablespoons of water, or enough to form the consistency of wallpaper paste.

Add the chicken strips and mix again. The batter should stick to each strip and coat them thoroughly. Set to one side.

Heat a 5cm depth of oil in a wok or large saucepan for 8–10 minutes until you can feel waves of heat come off with the palm of your hand. Using your hands, gently drop the chicken strips, one by one, into the hot oil, until the surface of the wok is covered, but make sure the strips do not touch.

Let the nuggets fry for 2–4 minutes, until they appear crisp and golden around the edges, then flip them gently and fry for another 2–4 minutes. Remove the nuggets with a slotted spoon and place in a colander set over a dish or frying pan. Drain the nuggets on plenty of kitchen paper and serve immediately with chilli sauce (page 236).

Steamed Eggs

KYET U PAUNG ကြက်ဥပေါင်း

As a child I'd regularly rush home from school, lift the lid of our rice cooker
and dig my spoon into the eggy bowl to hoover up a mouthful of this softly
luscious but simple dish. You don't need a rice cooker to make this – a
steamer will do or even (heaven forbid) a microwave!

The ultimate comfort food, *kyet u paung* goes perfectly either with a
bowl of fluffy steamed rice or, when sliced into wobbly golden slabs, in a
sandwich smeared with some mayonnaise – my favourite being the Japanese
Kewpie brand.

Serves 4

1 tablespoon ground arrowroot,
  or self-raising flour
1 tablespoon groundnut oil or
  other neutral-tasting oil
4 eggs
1 teaspoon fish sauce

Lightly whisk the arrowroot and 2 tablespoons of water together in a heatproof
bowl. Add the oil, eggs and fish sauce, and whisk again.

There are three ways you can cook this:

Rice cooker: If you're making rice anyway, place the bowl inside the
cooker on top of the rice for the last 10 minutes of cooking and it should
steam perfectly. This is the gentlest method and also gives the best
wibbly-wobbly texture.

Steamer: Steam with a cover for 15 minutes.

Microwave: Microwave at 75–80% of the full power, uncovered, for
5 minutes.

Whichever method you choose, the eggs should puff up like a cloud.

Duck Egg Curry

BE U CHET   ဘဲဥချက်

I'm a rampant carnivore, but even I can see that it would be better for the planet's future to go meat-free where possible and everyone can do it at least one day a week.

Therefore, I present to you my favourite vegetarian Burmese dish – egg curry aka *be u chet* (literally 'duck egg cooked'). Some people like to fry the peeled, hard-boiled eggs in turmeric-infused oil until they're golden and blistered all over. I usually don't have the patience, but it's definitely worth a try.

Serves 4

8 duck eggs or large hen's eggs

For the sauce
1 teaspoon tamarind paste or
   2.5cm cube tamarind block
   or 1 teaspoon lemon juice
½ bunch of coriander
2 tablespoons groundnut oil
   or other neutral-tasting oil
3 medium onions, diced
400g tin chopped tomatoes
6 curry leaves
1 tablespoon paprika
1 teaspoon ground turmeric
1 teaspoon chilli powder
1 teaspoon fish sauce
¼ teaspoon MSG or ½
   tablespoon chicken or
   vegetable bouillon

If using a tamarind block, place in a bowl with 100ml of just-boiled water and allow to soak for 10 minutes – it should break down into a thick paste. Remove the stones and the fibrous bits.

Chop off the stems from the coriander and mince them as finely as possible. Chop the leaves and reserve them for later.

Heat the oil in a saucepan, toss in the onions and coriander stems, and add the rest of the sauce ingredients. Cook this mixture down over a medium heat for 1 hour or until it breaks down into a sauce and then keep it simmering gently over a low heat.

Place the eggs in a saucepan, cover with cold water and heat over a high heat until the eggs start to boil and bubble furiously. Immediately turn the heat down to medium and simmer for 4 minutes. Remove from heat, drain and then submerge the eggs in cold, running water to stop them cooking. Peel the eggs and slice each in half – you should have yolks that are perfectly creamy. Stir the halves gently through the simmering sauce to coat. Scatter the egg curry with a handful of chopped coriander leaves and serve immediately with steamed rice and some crudités on the side such as cucumber slices or radishes.

Acacia Leaf Omelette

TSU BOKE KYET U KHAUK KYAW

Proper name *Acacia pennata*, known as *tsu boke* in Burmese and *cha om* in Thai, acacia leaves taste like heaven, but smell like absolute hell. My charming husband refers to them as 'poo weed'. In fact, the sulphurous vapours are so noxious that allegedly Thai people won't put them near mynah birds, lest the poor creatures become overwhelmed by fumes and drop dead.

The Burmese, Thai, Laotians and Cambodians all eat acacia leaves in pretty much the same way, either blanched and dipped into various sauces or fried up in an omelette.

The leaves need to be prepared carefully though – *tsu boke* literally means 'rotten thorn' in Burmese – but it's worth the trouble. Oh, and if you're wondering, acacia's bizarre stench totally disappears when it's cooked.

Serves 2

1 bunch of acacia leaves (*cha om*) (about 250g)
4 large eggs
1 heaped tablespoon plain flour
50ml milk
pinch of salt
¼ teaspoon MSG or ½ tablespoon chicken or vegetable bouillon
2 tablespoons groundnut oil or other neutral-tasting oil

Prepare the acacia leaves first. Rinse them gently in a colander, then pluck the fronds off carefully and discard the thorny stems. You should end up with a little pile of tender leaves.

Next whisk the eggs in a bowl with the flour, milk, salt and MSG until light and frothy.

Heat the oil in a frying pan over a high heat and pour in the egg mixture. As soon as the egg begins to set, strew the acacia leaves evenly over the top of the omelette and turn the heat down to medium. Allow to cook for 5 minutes, until the omelette is cooked most of the way through. Flip it so the leaf-covered side sets, too.

Finally slice the omelette into sections and serve on steaming rice.

Cook's Note
In Burma, this dish would be served alongside *ngapi yay-kyo* (page 204) or *ngapi kyaw* (page 211). In Thailand, it's eaten with *nam prik* (chilli dipping sauce). You can however substitute Japanese pickles or South-Asian pickles (*achar*) as they're easier to find in the UK.

Fish & Seafood

NGAR, PINLEZA

ငါး, ပင်လယ်စာ

The Irrawaddy River runs almost all the way through Burma, so practically every Burmese meal will contain river fish or prawns, even beyond fish sauce or shrimp paste. They might be simply fried, or served in a rich curry, in a spicy stir-fry, as a kind of jerky similar to the Icelandic *harðfiskur* or as a fragrant dish steamed with ginger and herbs, or even just some dried shrimp fried in a little oil – a favourite dish of my grandmother's when eaten with plain rice.

Burmese river prawns are sweeter than those from the sea, rivalling lobster for their size and flavour. Sadly, most of the biggest and best are exported, which makes them heinously expensive in Burma, but this means our prawns are legendary worldwide – my dad says that when friends visited Burmese ships to buy goods from the homeland (this was pre-Tilbury – see Back in Blighty, page 19), the sailors told them to bribe the port officials with a prawn, so they'd turn a blind eye to some of the more illicit packages. This sounds like an apocryphal tale to me, but my father swears that it's true!

Seafood is still not that common in land-locked parts of the country, especially Upper Burma. We even use the same word *khayu* for shellfish as we do for snails. When I was 10, we were invited to dinner by one of my mum's uncles and I was greatly alarmed to hear we were having a speciality known as *khayu khao swè*. Thankfully, the seafood noodles that appeared were delicious (that's also just reminded me that we call Tom Cruise, 'Tom Khayu' because we don't use 'R's in spoken Burmese). This means that people love to indulge in crab and lobster and other types of seafood when visiting beach resorts such as Ngwe Saung and Ngapali.

Fried Fish Curry

NGAR KYAW CHET ငါးကြော်ချက်

This dish is usually made with fish 'steaks' aka cutlets, but it is just as good with fillets or whole fish. The type of fish doesn't really matter either, as the luscious, spicy sauce is the thing, so it works equally well with, say, cod or salmon.

Serves 2–4

For the fish
1 teaspoon salt
2 tablespoons plain flour
1 teaspoon ground turmeric
¼ teaspoon MSG or ½
　tablespoon chicken or
　vegetable bouillon
1 whole sea bream or sea bass,
　or 4 basa or catfish slices (sold
　frozen in Asian supermarkets)
120ml groundnut oil or other
　neutral-tasting oil, plus an
　extra 2 tablespoons

For the sauce
4 medium onions, sliced thinly
⅓ standard tin of chopped
　tomatoes (about 135g)
3 fresh tomatoes, diced
1 tablespoon fish sauce
¼ teaspoon MSG or 1 tablespoon
　chicken or vegetable bouillon

For the garnish
2 finger chillies
handful of coriander leaves,
　chopped

Mix the salt, flour, turmeric and MSG in a large dish, then add the fish. Turn the fish over in the seasonings, making sure it is thoroughly coated. Heat the 120ml of oil in a wok or large frying pan over a high heat until sizzling, then carefully add the fish. Fry for 2–3 minutes on each side. Remove the fish using a slotted spoon and set to one side on a dish.

In the same wok, heat the remaining 2 tablespoons of oil over a high heat and add the sauce ingredients. Fry for 5 minutes, tossing and stirring regularly. Turn the heat down to medium-high and continue to fry for another 10 minutes. Add the fish and the chillies, and toss gently in the sauce. Dish up on a platter, scatter the coriander leaves on top and serve with steamed rice.

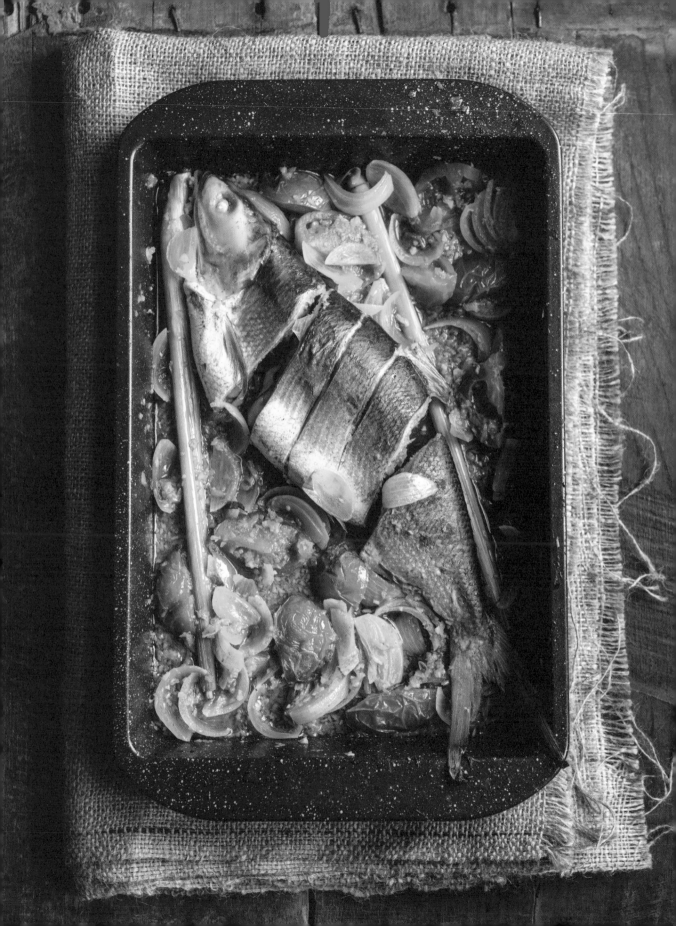

Tender Steamed Hilsa

NGA THALAUT PAUNG   ငါးသလောက်ပေါင်း

Hilsa (also known as *ilish*) is a bony freshwater fish that melts to deliciousness when cooked slowly, so that you can eat it, bones and all. It's pretty hard to come by in the UK, but mackerel is similar in terms of flavour, as is frozen milkfish, which is available in Asian supermarkets (although watch out for the bones as milkfish bones don't disintegrate in the same way as hilsas). My mum is a fan of *nga thalaut paung* but rarely makes it, so when I cooked it for her for the first time, it was wonderful to see her smile and say it tasted just the way she remembered.

Serves 4

2 mackerel, cleaned and gutted, heads and tails removed (see Cook's Note)
2 medium onions, peeled

For the marinade
200ml vinegar
2 tablespoons fish sauce
1 teaspoon ground turmeric
1 teaspoon paprika
1 teaspoon mild chilli powder
1 teaspoon salt

For the sauce
2 spring onions
3cm piece of ginger, peeled
6 garlic cloves, peeled
4 tablespoons groundnut oil or other neutral-tasting oil
2 tomatoes, cut into wedges
2 lemongrass stalks

Place the fish in a container with a lid and add the marinade ingredients and rub the ingredients all over the fish. Cover and chill for at least 2 hours or overnight.

Slice one of the onions and set to one side.

Meanwhile, blitz the other onion, the spring onions, ginger and garlic in a blender or food processor to a rough paste.

Heat the oil in a deep saucepan, fish kettle or stockpot with a close-fitting lid over a medium heat. Add the paste and sauté for at least 5 minutes until the onion and garlic become fragrant. Add the fish and its marinade, the sliced onion, tomatoes, lemongrass and 500ml of water. Cover with the lid, turn the heat to high and bring to the boil. Turn the heat down to low and allow to simmer gently for 2 hours until the fish falls apart and the liquid reduces to a sticky sauce. Serve with steamed rice.

Cook's Note
You could also make this in the oven in a lidded casserole dish (or baking dish covered in aluminium foil). Cook the fish in an oven preheated to 160°C/140°C Fan/Gas Mark 3 for 2 hours. At the end of that time, pour the liquid into a saucepan (keep the fish warm in the oven) and cook over a high heat for 10 minutes until reduced to a sticky sauce.

You can also leave their heads and tails on for decorative purposes, as pictured.

Po Po's Pilchard & Tomato Curry

NGAR THITDAR CHET   ငါးသေတ္တာချက်

My parents came to the UK in 1979 and, as hospital doctors, they couldn't afford to take us back to Burma for a while, so when I was three, my grandparents came to live with us for a year.

My *Po Po* was so tall that when he sat down, his sarong (known in Burmese as a *paso*) could form a makeshift swing for me, and I have vivid memories of sitting in it whilst snacking on sunflower seeds. As I sat there, he'd recount stories of life in the British Army, when Burma was still part of the British Empire. During his time in the forces, he became fond of English food like baked beans and corned beef, which he'd call bully beef, so we'd take him precious supplies when we were finally able to visit him in turn. *Po Po* was also a fan of tinned fish, and they were the basis of this speedy dish he'd invented using army rations and local Burmese produce – a pilchard and tomato curry, which sounds dubious but was delicious. He passed away a good few years ago, so whenever I miss him, I make this curry and remember swinging in his sarong.

Serves 4-6

small bunch of coriander, stems
    and leaves separated
4 tablespoons groundnut oil
    or other neutral-tasting oil
1 teaspoon paprika
1 large onion, sliced into rings
400g tin pilchards in tomato
    sauce
1 teaspoon salt
1 teaspoon ground black pepper

Pound the coriander stems with 1 tablespoon of water using a mortar and pestle (or blitz in a food processor or blender) to form a smooth paste. Roughly chop the coriander leaves and set to one side.

Heat the oil in a wok or frying pan over a medium-high heat. Add the coriander stem paste and the paprika. Stir-fry for 4–5 minutes until fragrant, and then add the onion. Continue to stir-fry for another 4-5 minutes, until the onion softens and becomes fragrant, then add the pilchards, including their tomato sauce, followed by salt and pepper and a splash of water to loosen the sauce. Stir-fry for another 4–5 minutes, breaking the pilchards up into large chunks as you go. At this point, the onion rings should be translucent but still retain some bite.

Scatter the coriander leaves on top and serve immediately with steamed rice.

Red Prawn Curry

PAZUN SEE-PYAN   ပုစွန်ဆီပြန်

I've always been obsessed with prawns – little ones, big ones and all the ones in between – but I didn't realise how magnificent they could be until I first tasted this prawn curry in Burma. Somehow, the savoury-sweetness seemed intensified, and I remember licking my plate clean. I discovered that there was a magical substance in the heads of prawns known in Burmese as *pazun see* (prawn oil) that was responsible for this extraordinary rush of prawny goodness – you can even buy jars of this precious elixir to mix straight into your rice – and I vowed to replicate this wondrous curry back in England as soon as I could.

Serves 4
or 6 if part of a sharing menu

4 tablespoons groundnut oil or other neutral-tasting oil
2 medium onions, roughly chopped
4 garlic cloves, peeled and sliced
2 tablespoons tomato purée
1 teaspoon paprika
½ teaspoon mild chilli powder
1 kg of the largest raw tiger or king prawns you can find with shells and heads still on
¼ teaspoon ground turmeric
½ teaspoon salt
1 tablespoon fish sauce

Heat the oil in a wok or saucepan over a high heat. Add the onions and garlic and fry for 5 minutes, until fragrant. Add the tomato purée, paprika, chilli powder and 500ml of water, and bring to the boil. Turn the heat down to medium and simmer for 30–45 minutes, stirring frequently, until the onions and garlic break down completely, the sauce is reduced and you see a ring of oil appear around the inner edges of the wok (known as *see-pyan* or 'the oil returns').

Meanwhile, take the head off one prawn and inside the head you will see a reddish/yellow blob (known as *pazun see* or 'prawn oil' in Burmese). Carefully scoop the prawn oil out of the prawn head (it's okay if any grey gunk comes with it) and add it to the sauce. Repeat with the rest of the prawn heads, and discard the heads (see Cook's Note).

Next, carefully remove the shells and tails from the prawns and cut a slit down their backs to butterfly the prawns slightly. Discard any black gunk (veins), which you'll find when doing this. Rub the cleaned prawns with the turmeric and the salt and leave to marinate for 5 minutes.

Heat the sauce over a medium-high heat and stir through the prawn oil that you added above. Now add the fish sauce and prawns and simmer for 10 minutes, or until the prawns are pink and cooked through.

Serve with steamed rice.

Cook's Note
Known as *tomalley* in crabs and lobsters, *pazun see* is needed to give this dish its proper, intensely prawny flavour. That's why it's essential you use prawns that still have their heads still attached. You can, however, leave the heads on a few prawns for decorative purposes, as pictured.

Spiced Crab Curry

GANAN HIN ကကန်းဟင်း

Crab is considered a rare treat in Burma and so it is usually cooked alive and eaten whole to do it justice. I am, however, a massive wuss and will usually use frozen crab claws, or occasionally frozen blue swimming crabs from the Asian supermarket. This particular dish is great with rice and leafy vegetables such as Straw Mushroom and Water Spinach Stir-fry (page 188), but it can also be eaten with plain noodles or even fluffy breads similar to Singapore chilli crab.

Serves 4

2 medium onions, roughly chopped
4 garlic cloves, peeled
3cm piece of ginger, peeled
½ bunch of coriander, stems and leaves separated
4 tablespoons groundnut oil or other neutral-tasting oil
1 tomato, sliced into wedges
6 curry leaves
1 teaspoon paprika
½ teaspoon mild chilli powder
¼ teaspoon ground turmeric
1 tablespoon fish sauce
750g cooked crab claws
150g cooked white crabmeat
2 finger chillies
½ teaspoon salt
2 spring onions, green and white parts, shredded, to garnish

Blitz the onions, garlic, ginger and coriander stems in a food processor or blender to a rough paste. Set to one side.

Heat the oil in a wok or saucepan over a high heat. Add the onion paste and fry for 5 minutes until fragrant. Add the tomato, curry leaves, paprika, chilli powder, turmeric and 400ml of water, and bring to the boil. Turn the heat down to medium-low and simmer for 2 hours, until the sauce is completely reduced and you see a ring of oil appear around the inner edges of the wok (known as *see-pyan* or 'the oil returns'). Add a little extra water if it looks like the curry might stick at any point before the time is up.

Turn the heat up to medium-high, then add the fish sauce and crab claws, and simmer for 5 minutes, just to warm through. Add the crabmeat and simmer for another 5 minutes, then stir in the chillies and salt, to taste. Serve with steamed rice and topped with coriander leaves and the shredded spring onions.

Vegetables

HIN-THI HIN-YWET

ဟင်းသီးဟင်းရွက်

The variety of fresh vegetables in Burma means that we can never resist adding at least one vegetable dish to every meal, however fond we are of meat.

Leafy vegetables like water morning glory might be stir-fried simply with garlic, squashes merit a more intense treatment and beans of every variety are stewed, fried or steamed.

Some of the ingredients could be considered a little unusual, but necessity is the mother of invention and it is perfectly acceptable to substitute so long as the spirit remains the same.

Sprouted Yellow Peas with Onions

PE PYOTE   ပဲပြုတ်

Mohinga (page 107) may be considered our national breakfast, but these boiled yellow peas served with oiled rice or Golden Sticky Rice (page 97) are actually the most common way to start the day, and the one that I always looked forward to when staying with my grandparents in Mandalay. Sprouting the yellow peas is easy enough – though it takes a little patience – but you can substitute dried marrowfat peas, which only require an overnight soak, and cook them the same way. The peas are also delicious with Indian breads such as *poori* or *chapati*.

Serves 6–8

250g dried whole yellow peas
1 teaspoon bicarbonate of soda
2 tablespoons soft light
  brown sugar
2 tablespoons groundnut oil
  or other neutral-tasting oil
1 teaspoon salt

For the fried onions
2 tablespoons groundnut oil
  or other neutral-tasting oil
½ medium onion, sliced
¼ teaspoon ground turmeric

Place the peas in a bowl with plenty of water and soak overnight.

The next day, drain the peas. Line a colander with a double layer of moistened kitchen paper. Add the peas and then cover them with another double layer of moistened kitchen paper and leave somewhere dark at room temperature. You could also use a wet muslin cloth. The aim is to get the peas to sprout – so make sure the kitchen paper does not dry out (remoisten it 2–3 times a day). If it begins to smell frowsy or fusty, rinse the peas and change the kitchen paper.

After 2–3 days (depending on the weather conditions), the peas should have 1cm-long sprouts. Rinse them gently to avoid knocking the sprouts off and then place in a large bowl. Scatter ½ teaspoon of bicarbonate of soda over the peas and gently mix through with your hands. Cover with water and then leave for 1 hour to allow the peas to soften.

Drain the peas and place them in a large saucepan or stockpot. Add the remaining ½ teaspoon of bicarbonate of soda, the sugar, the oil and enough water to generously submerge the peas – about 1.25 litres.

Place a metal colander or steamer basket in the saucepan so it sits on top of the peas. This will stop the skins and sprouts breaking off and floating away. Turn the heat up to high and bring to the boil, turn the heat down to medium, cover with a lid and simmer for 1½ hours or until the water has completely disappeared.

Meanwhile, make the fried onions. Heat the oil in a wok or large frying pan over a medium-high heat and then add the onion and turmeric. Fry for 15 minutes, until wilted and some have browned. Set to one side.

Now check the peas for tenderness – they should be soft and yielding but still retain their shape. Toss the peas gently with the salt and fried onions, making sure not to knock the sprouts off. Serve with golden sticky rice (page 97) or Indian breads.

Roselle Leaves with Bamboo Shoots

CHIN BAUNG KYAW   ချဉ်ပေါင်ကြော်

This is probably our most iconic vegetable dish – it encapsulates the flavours we love best, as it's sour, spicy and savoury all in one. Roselle can be found in South Asian supermarkets labelled as *gongura*, but sorrel makes a fine substitute and is easier to come by. You can even swap in a handful of chopped rhubarb stalks mixed with spinach for a similar taste and effect. If you want to have this as a main, use fresh prawns as this will make it more substantial, but for a side dish, use the dried shrimp.

Serves 2-4

1 large bunch of fresh roselle or
   sorrel leaves (about 400g)
140g tinned bamboo shoot
   strips, drained
90ml groundnut oil or other
   neutral-tasting oil
¼ teaspoon ground turmeric
1 medium onion, sliced
6 garlic cloves, sliced
1 medium ripe tomato, diced
3 finger chillies
3 tablespoons dried shrimp,
   or 10 raw king prawns, shells
   on (optional)
1 tablespoon fish sauce
½ teaspoon salt

Wash the roselle and pick off the leaves. Cut the bamboo shoots into fine shreds using a knife or a mandoline.

Heat the oil in a wok or frying pan over a medium-high heat and add the turmeric, onion and garlic. Fry for 5 minutes, until the onions become fragrant and golden.

Add the roselle leaves, bamboo and tomato. Stir-fry for another 15 minutes until the roselle has completely wilted to a mossy green. Add the whole chillies, dried shrimp, if using, fish sauce and salt, and simmer for another 10 minutes until you see a ring of oil appear around the inner edges of the wok (known as *see-pyan* or 'the oil returns'). Serve with steamed rice.

Cook's Note
If you can't find roselle or sorrel, substitute with a mix of 200g chopped rhubarb and 200g spinach.

Aubergine Pan-sticker Curry

KHAYAN THI OH-GAT   ခရမ်းသီးအိုးကပ်

I've never been too keen on aubergine, as frankly I'm suspicious of its texture, but there are two ways that I will gladly eat it. One is the Japanese dish known as *nasu dengaku* (miso-glazed aubergines) and the other, this Burmese dish where aubergine is slow-cooked until it sticks to the pan (hence the name, a literal translation). If you can track down finger or baby aubergines, so much the better, as you'll completely avoid the bitterness you sometimes get with the larger version.

Serves 4

2 aubergines or 6 finger
  aubergines
200g tinned chopped tomatoes
2 medium onions, diced
1 tablespoon shrimp paste
  (*belacan*)
2 finger chillies, topped and
  tailed and each chopped into
  3 pieces
1 tablespoon salted peanuts,
  crushed, or 1 tablespoon
  peanut butter
handful of chopped coriander
  leaves
150ml groundnut oil or other
  neutral-tasting oil
¼ teaspoon MSG or ½
  tablespoon chicken or
  vegetable bouillon
1 teaspoon salt
1 teaspoon sugar
1 teaspoon ground turmeric
1 tablespoon paprika

Remove both ends of each aubergine and then slice them into 2cm-width rounds. If using finger aubergines, slice them into halves. Wash thoroughly. Add to a large bowl with the rest of the ingredients and mix by hand, massaging the spices into the aubergine.

Place everything in a large frying pan or wok over a high heat and cover with a lid. Fry for 10 minutes, until you hear 'bubbling', then remove the lid and give them a stir.

Put the lid back on and turn the heat down to medium. Leave to simmer for 15 minutes until the aubergines start to wilt and then remove the lid and stir again.

Put the lid back on and leave to simmer for another 15 minutes, until the ingredients have softened, then remove the lid and stir again. Reduce the heat to medium-low and allow to cook for 1 hour, or until the curry sticks to the pan. Serve.

Braised Butter Beans

PE GYI HNAT

This is an easy side dish that is greater than the sum of its parts. Usually made using *lablab* (aka hyacinth) beans – the *pe gyi* in the name – the secret is to fry the beans until they're completely dry and parts of them start to stick to the pan and go a caramelised brown. As this is quite dry, I like to serve it with a sauced dish such as Paddy-planter's Relish (page 208) or soup.

Serves 2 as a main
or 4 as a side

90ml groundnut oil or other
   neutral-tasting oil
½ teaspoon ground turmeric
2 medium onions, sliced
400g tin butter beans, white
   butter beans or cannellini
   beans, drained
1 teaspoon salt
1 tablespoon fish sauce

Heat the oil in a saucepan over a high heat. Add the turmeric to the oil and allow to sizzle for a few seconds. Now add the onions, turn the heat down to medium and fry for 10 minutes until the onions have wilted and some have crisped up.

Add the beans, salt and fish sauce, and fry for another 10–15 minutes until the beans have browned a little and are dry. Serve with golden sticky rice (page 97) or as a side dish to steamed rice and a main curry.

Golden Pumpkin Curry

SHWE HPAYONE-THI CHET ရွှေဖရုံသီးချက်

I'm one of those terrible carnivores and I strongly believe in the (semi-joking) Burmese affliction of *a-thar ma-sar yat-de yaw-ga* i.e. 'the illness caused by the failure to eat meat'. However, if this gorgeous pumpkin curry is on the table, for once I'll barely twitch. You can use any winter squash you like – it's very good made with kabocha squash or crown prince. If you want to make this a vegetarian dish, you can swap out the shrimp paste and fish sauce for an equal amount of Japanese miso.

Serves 2 as a main
or 4–6 as a side

90ml groundnut oil or other neutral-tasting oil
1 teaspoon ground turmeric
1 teaspoon ground coriander
1 teaspoon ground cumin
1 teaspoon paprika
8 fresh or dried curry leaves
2 medium onions, sliced
1 spring onion, green and white parts, shredded
4 garlic cloves, sliced
2cm piece of ginger, peeled and sliced
1 butternut or kabocha squash, peeled and cubed
1 tablespoon sugar
1 teaspoon shrimp paste (*belacan*)
2 tablespoons fish sauce

Heat the oil in a saucepan over a high heat. Add the turmeric, coriander, cumin, paprika and curry leaves to the oil and allow to sizzle for a few seconds.

Now turn the heat down to medium and add the onions, spring onion, garlic and ginger and fry for 10 minutes, until fragrant and the onions have wilted and some have crisped up.

Add the squash, sugar, shrimp paste and 300ml of water. Stir well. Cover and cook for 25 minutes, or until the squash is tender. Add the fish sauce, stir again and serve with steamed rice.

Straw Mushroom & Water Spinach Stir-fry

HMO GAZUN-YWET KYAW မှိုကန်စွန်းရွက်ကြော်

Straw mushrooms are fascinating as they look like little lightbulbs – you may have seen them pop up in Thai dishes such as *tom yum* soup. They stay tender when cooked, so combined with the perky water spinach aka water morning glory (stop laughing at the back) the whole dish has a pleasing bounce to it. You can swap in oyster mushrooms and baby spinach for less spring but a similar taste.

Serves 4

400g tin straw mushrooms

1 bunch of water spinach (*ong choy/kang kung*) (about 500g)

4 tablespoons groundnut oil or other neutral-tasting oil

8 garlic cloves, sliced

1 onion, sliced

2 tablespoons light soy sauce

¼ teaspoon MSG or ½ tablespoon chicken or vegetable bouillon

Drain the straw mushrooms and rinse them in a colander. If they are whole, slice them in half. Lay the bunch of spinach on a chopping board and chop it into 4 lengthways.

Heat 4 tablespoons of oil in a wok or deep frying pan over a medium-high heat. Add the garlic and onion and stir-fry for 5 minutes, until fragrant. Turn the heat to high and add the water spinach, mushrooms, soy sauce and MSG. Stir-fry for another 8–10 minutes, until the spinach wilts and then serve.

Cook's Note

If you can't find water spinach or tinned mushrooms (both of which are rather robust), you can substitute baby spinach and oyster mushrooms and reduce the frying time in the final step of the recipe to 4–5 minutes.

Creamed Corn with Onions

PYAUNG-HPU KYAW

Condensed milk is the secret and perhaps startling ingredient in this recipe for Burmese creamed corn. Although I'm not sweet-toothed, I used to hoover this stuff up as a child and my kids now do the same. Use double cream instead if you really must, but it's worth trying it the way it should be, as pure comfort food (just try not to think about *garmonbozia* while you're at it). Note that two different types of corn are needed here to get the texture of Burmese corn (which comes in all sorts of different colours). This dish makes a good accompaniment to Duck Egg Curry (page 160) or try it as a topping for toast.

Serves 4
as a side

2 onions, 1 sliced and 1 diced
4 tablespoons groundnut oil or neutral-tasting oil
250g (or approximate weight) tinned sweetcorn kernels in unsalted, unsweetened water
250g frozen sweetcorn kernels
1 heaped tablespoon tapioca starch mixed with 3 tablespoons water to form a paste
1 tablespoon condensed milk or double cream

First, make the fried onion garnish. Squeeze the sliced onion with your hands so you get as much juice out as possible and discard this juice (I find microwaving the onion slices for a minute makes this job much easier).

Heat 2 tablespoons of oil in a wok or frying pan over a high heat. Turn the heat down to medium and fry the sliced onions for 15 minutes, and then turn the heat back up to high and fry for another 5 minutes, until browned and beginning to crisp up a little. Transfer to a small bowl and set to one side.

Briefly blitz all the sweetcorn (including the liquid from the tinned sweetcorn) in a blender or food processor until most but not all of the kernels break down into a mush.

Heat the remaining 2 tablespoons of oil in the same wok or pan used for the onions over a medium heat. Fry the diced onion for 10 minutes until translucent. Add the blitzed sweetcorn, the tapioca paste and the condensed milk to the wok, stir thoroughly and fry for another 10 minutes.

Serve warm, topped with the fried onions as a side dish.

Cook's Note
You may find you make more fried onions than needed for this dish, but they make a tasty all-round garnish – try them sprinkled on top of noodles and salads.

Pickles & Chutneys

A-CHIN, THANAT
အချဉ်သနပ်

Pickles are a near obsession for most people in Burma. They will toss them into most noodle dishes with wilful abandon, dash them into curries and salads and will often eat them straight from the pickle jar. As you know, I'm part Shan, an ethnic group who primarily live in a rural, hilly region in Burma known as the Shan State. Traditionally tall and fair, and cousins to the Dai people in Thailand, the Shan are incredibly fond of pickles (and noodles and pork – often the three in combination), so you could say that pickling is in my blood.

Our pickles add life, colour, flavour and most importantly texture to every dish – there is nothing quite like the occasional crunch of pickled leek bulbs in a bowl of noodle soup.

Some pickles, including the classic Shan pickle known as *Mon-nyin chin*, will take a while to develop the sour, pungent kick you crave, although it is always worth the wait. Others are ready in minutes, delivering instant tangy satisfaction.

Shan Mustard Green Pickle

MON-NYIN CHIN   မုန်ညင်းချဉ်

Mon-nyin chin is the most popular pickle in Burma and is not dissimilar to Korean kimchi. It features as a garnish for many Shan dishes such as Shan Noodles (page 114) and is even eaten as a kind of salad mixed with sliced raw onions, Crispy Noodles (page 239) and a dash of dark soy sauce. The name literally means 'mustard green pickle', hence my translation, but it generally refers to a wide range of pickled vegetables.

    The most classic form comprises a mix of mustard greens, carrots, baby leek bulbs, garlic chive roots and Chinese artichokes. The last three can be hard to find in this country (Chinese artichokes particularly), although you can use jarred or tinned pickled leeks from Asian supermarkets or pearl onions as I have below, and my parents grow their own garlic chives just for the roots, which are also eaten with Shan Sour Rice (page 102).

Fills a 1 litre jar (approx.)

2 large carrots, diced
  (about 250g)
1 small pak choi (about 150g),
  shredded
1 bunch of mustard greens
  (about 150g), shredded
3 tablespoons soft brown sugar
1 tablespoon paprika
1 tablespoon ground turmeric
1 tablespoon crushed
  fennel seeds
1 tablespoon salt
1 tablespoon rice flour
1 teaspoon chilli powder
200g pickled pearl onions or
  pickled leeks, drained but
  reserve 50ml pickling liquid
  from the jar

Mix all the ingredients (except the onion pickling liquid) thoroughly in a large bowl. Pack as tightly as possible into a sterilised jar leaving a 1–2cm gap at the top. Pour in the reserved pickling liquid to completely cover the surface of the vegetables.

Seal the jar and leave at room temperature to ferment for 2 days and then refrigerate. The pickle will be ready to eat in a week and keeps for a month in the fridge.

Shan Cauliflower & Carrot Pickle

PAN MON-LAR CHIN   ပန်းမုန်လာချဉ်

This recipe is for one of my favourite overnight pickles, using cauliflower and carrot, both of which are hard to come by in Lower Burma, but plentiful in the Shan State. Although, of course, carrots and cauliflowers aren't rare in the UK, it may be tricky to get hold of perilla seeds, which are the actual pickling spice used (known as *Shan hnan* in Burmese, which means 'Shan sesame'). I find, however, that black mustard seeds are an excellent substitute in terms of both texture and flavour. The vinegar that's traditionally used is a sweetish by-product from the manufacture of palm toddy, but again, malt vinegar works well instead.

Fills a 1 litre jar (approx.)

1 large cauliflower, broken
   into florets
2 large carrots, sliced into
   thin half moons
1 heaped tablespoon
   caster sugar
75ml malt vinegar
6 garlic cloves
2.5cm piece of ginger
1 tablespoon groundnut oil
   or other neutral-tasting oil
1 heaped tablespoon mild
   chilli powder
1 tablespoon black
   mustard seeds

Put the cauliflower and carrots in a large plastic bowl with the sugar and the vinegar. Mix everything well, cover and leave overnight in the fridge.

Remove the bowl of carrots and cauliflower from the fridge and have it ready next to the hob.

Chop the garlic and ginger roughly, leaving the skins on. Part of the flavour of this pickle comes from the skins – you can pick the bits out afterwards.

Heat the oil in a large frying pan over a high heat until sizzling, then add the garlic and ginger. Fry for a minute, add the chilli powder and the mustard seeds, then stir-fry for another minute. At this point, the seeds should start to pop and dance in the pan a little bit, and everything should smell fragrant.

Pick up the frying pan with both hands – being careful not to burn yourself – and pour the sizzling oil and all the bits in it onto the cauliflower and carrot. Mix thoroughly to 'cook' the pickled vegetables. Your spicy Shan cauliflower and carrot pickle is immediately ready to eat. It will keep in a jar or sealed container for a couple of days, after which point it will lose its crunch.

Cook's Note
This Shan pickle is traditionally eaten in Burma with noodles and rice, but it also works in sandwiches and with hot and cold meats. Think of it as a type of piccalilli or relish. You can have it as part of a ploughman's lunch, with a pork pie, on a hot dog, in a burger … the list goes on.

Quick Rainbow Pickle

THEEZOHN THANAT   သီးစုံသနပ်

This is pretty much the Burmese version of South Asian *achaar*, which you'll probably know better as the precursor to piccalilli. The difference is that *theezohn thanat* (literally 'all the vegetables chutney') is ready in almost an instant. Because of its Indian spicing, it makes a fine accompaniment for Indian-influenced dishes such as the Burmese Masala Chicken (page 151) and Goat and Split Pea Curry (page 138), but it's also excellent eaten in the same way as piccalilli – with cold meats, or a pork pie or as part of a ploughman's lunch.

Makes 750g

100g green beans, trimmed
200g cauliflower florets
1 medium carrot, halved
   and sliced
⅓ cucumber or 3 mini
   cucumbers, sliced
6 radishes, halved
6 garlic cloves, sliced
100ml malt vinegar
1 tablespoon caster sugar
1 teaspoon salt
3 tablespoons groundnut oil
   or other neutral-tasting oil
1 tablespoon mustard seeds
1 tablespoon ground cumin
1 teaspoon coriander seeds
1 teaspoon ground turmeric
½ teaspoon chilli flakes

Chop each bean into three pieces and place in a saucepan with the cauliflower and carrot. Pour a kettle of boiling water over the vegetables and leave to stand for a minute. Drain thoroughly and place in a large non-metallic bowl with the cucumber, radishes and garlic. Pour over the vinegar, add the sugar and salt, and mix the ingredients together with your hands. Leave to marinate for 15 minutes.

Heat the oil in a frying pan over a high heat. Add all the spices, turn the heat down to medium and allow to sizzle. As soon as the mustard and coriander seeds start to pop, remove the pan from the heat and pour the spiced oil over the marinated vegetables. When cool enough to handle, use your hands to toss the vegetables and oil. It's ready to eat immediately or store in a jar or tub in the fridge for 3 days. Serve as a side dish.

Pickled Beansprouts

PE DI CHIN

This the simplest pickle in Burma – the people's pickle, as it were – and it will appear on the table in a small metal dish at most home-style Burmese restaurants known as *htamin-zain* (literally 'rice shops'). My favourite cousin was a bit of a snob about this pickle, because it was so rudimentary and given away for free (and bear in mind that beansprouts in Burma are skinny, straggly little things). She was frequently appalled that I'd always polish it off with gusto along with my rice and curry. It may well be very basic, but it's genuinely rather good. I've given the traditional method for making the pickle, but you can also just whisk a teaspoon of rice flour with the water rather than soaking actual rice grains and it will work just as well.

Serves 6-8
as a condiment

80g uncooked white rice
1 teaspoon salt
¼ teaspoon ground turmeric
1 x standard packet of
   beansprouts (approx. 350g)

Put the rice in a large bowl and add 500ml of water. Rinse the rice in the water, swishing with a spoon or your hands to get the water as cloudy as possible and then leave the rice to soak for 1 hour. Pour the rice water into another bowl, but reserve the rice itself for another dish. Add the salt and turmeric to the rice water and whisk together.

Wash the beansprouts, drain, and place in a sterilised jar or container with a lid. Pour the turmeric rice water over the beansprouts, pressing the beansprouts down to submerge them thoroughly.

Seal the jar and leave at room temperature for 2 days and then refrigerate and eat within a week. Serve as a side dish with any curry and rice, or even as a garnish for any noodle dish.

Condiments, Relishes & Dips

HIN-YAN

ဟင်းရံ

The Burmese are absolutely crazy about condiments, relishes and dips. There is always room on the plate for some shrimp relish, anchovy dip, *balachaung* or salsa. For us, it adds that little bit of magic to every meal and is occasionally more thrilling than the main event.

Add some blanched vegetables or crudités, such as green mango or cucumber slices and honestly, often, you'll need nothing more.

Ngapi is almost literally the lifeblood of Burma – for much more on this iconic ingredient that forms the base of many of our condiments please refer to the Food of Burma on pages 25–29.

Anchovy Dip

NGAPI YAY-KYO ငပိရည်ကြို

Ngapi yay-kyo (literally 'boiled *ngapi* water') is the thin, spicy cousin to the Italian *bagna cauda*, and it is served in a similar way. A small bowl of *ngapi yay-kyo*, the more pungent the better and drizzled with chilli oil, will be served surrounded by a panoply of vegetables comprising whatever looks good that day – so you might have salad leaves such as pennywort, pickled and bitter herbs such as neem, blanched winged beans, bamboo shoot tips and Thai eggplants and crudités like white cabbage and cucumber.

This sauce is fundamental to any meal in a Yangon home, forming part of the traditional table along with curries, soups, stir-fries, fritters and rice. Throughout the meal, diners will dip their chosen morsels into the *ngapi yay-kyo*, as well as splashing some of the sauce directly onto their rice.

Serves 4-6

30g anchovies preserved in oil
(drained weight)
2 tablespoons shrimp paste
(*belacan*)
1 tablespoon fish sauce
pinch of ground turmeric
6 garlic cloves, peeled
1 tablespoon dried shrimp
2 dried red chillies
1 green finger chilli
few coriander leaves, to garnish

Add the drained anchovies, shrimp paste, fish sauce, turmeric and 3 of the garlic cloves to a saucepan with 400ml of water. Bring to the boil over a high heat and then turn the heat down to medium and simmer for 30 minutes. Strain the anchovy sauce into a bowl, discarding the solids. Set the sauce to one side to cool.

Meanwhile pound the rest of the garlic, shrimps and chillies using a pestle and mortar until you have as smooth a paste as possible (or do this in a food processor). Mix with the anchovy sauce and pour into a serving dish. Top with coriander leaves and serve with crudités.

Pounded Fish Paste Relish

NGAPI HTAUNG ငပိထောင်း

Ngapi htaung is my favourite condiment, the name literally meaning 'ngapi pounded'. Similar to the Thai *nam phrik kapi*, it's simply *ngapi* crushed with fresh chillies, dried shrimp and garlic to a funky, spicy paste using a pestle and mortar. Sometimes made with the addition of minced raw onion, *ngapi htaung* packs a bit of a punch, so it's served with cooling fruits and vegetables such as green mango and cucumber. To eat it, add a healthy squeeze of fresh lime juice to thin, then dip in your vegetables, or mix it with rice.

Serves 4-6

25g shrimp paste (*belacan*)
30g dried shrimp (about a handful)
2 finger chillies
6 garlic cloves, skin on
1 tablespoon groundnut oil or other neutral-tasting oil
juice of ½ lime

Cut out 2 pieces of aluminium foil, measuring 15cm × 15cm. Spread the shrimp paste onto one piece of foil, leaving a 1cm border. Sprinkle the dried shrimp onto the layer of shrimp paste. Carefully fold the foil in half, and crimp the edges so it forms a flat, rectangular packet.

Wrap the chillies and the garlic in the other piece of foil. Put both foil parcels over an open flame for 5 minutes until the shrimp paste smells toasted and fragrant and the garlic and the chillies are slightly charred. (You can also do this under a very hot grill, in which case, keep the chillies and garlic unwrapped and simply sit them on the foil.)

Peel off the garlic skin and put the garlic flesh into a large mortar or a small food processor or blender along with the contents of the foil packets. Add the oil and 2 tablespoons of water, and grind/blitz everything into a rough paste.

With a rubber spatula, scrape every bit of the paste into a small bowl. Stir the lime juice into the paste, mixing well.

Serve the finished *ngapi htaung* as a condiment with steamed rice or crudités such as slices of green mango or cucumber with extra lime on the side.

Paddy-planter's Relish

KAUK-SIKE NGAPI CHET ကောက်စိုက်ငပိချက်

This is a variant of Mandalay's most famous *ngapi*-based dish known as
ngapi chet or 'cooked *ngapi*'. It's basically a curry and would be a regular
feature in the households of those that worked in the rice paddy fields,
hence the name of *kauk-sike*, which literally means 'pick, sow' i.e. the act
of transplanting rice seedlings by hand.

Serves 4-6
as a side dish

50g tin anchovy fillets in oil
3 tablespoons groundnut oil
  or other neutral-tasting oil
¼ teaspoon ground turmeric
1 teaspoon paprika
1 onion, sliced
6 garlic cloves, chopped
1 teaspoon shrimp paste
  (*belacan*)
3 tomatoes, sliced or 250g cherry
  or baby plum tomatoes, pierced
2 green finger chillies, halved
1 spring onion, chopped into 4
1 tablespoon fish sauce

Pour the oil from the anchovy tin into a saucepan (reserving the anchovies in
the tin) and add the groundnut oil. Heat on high and then add the turmeric and
paprika and allow to sizzle for a few seconds. Reduce the heat to medium and
add the onion and garlic. Fry for 5 minutes, until softened. Add the anchovies,
shrimp paste and tomatoes. Fill the now-empty anchovy tin with water and
then pour this water into the pan. Repeat.

Stir well and then turn the heat up to high. Bring everything to the boil and
cook for 5 minutes, stirring constantly. Reduce the heat to medium and cook
for another 15 minutes. Add the chillies, then cook for another 5 minutes. Stir
in the spring onion and fish sauce, then serve as a side dish with a main curry
and rice, or with a selection of raw vegetables as a dip.

Balachaung

NGAPI KYAW / BALACHAUNG KYAW   ငါးပိကြော် / ဘာလချောင်ကြော်

The most famous condiment for rice is a *sambal* known as *ngapi kyaw* or *balachaung*, which is a fishy base made from shrimp and *belacan* fried slowly with tamarind, salt, onions and garlic. Your home may reek for a while afterwards, but it's so worth it.

It's usually served as a condiment to supplement curries, but a big spoonful of *ngapi kyaw* on top of a plate of hot rice is also a quick and easy meal that's popular among people of all ages, especially students. Poorer households will also often have *ngapi kyaw* as their only dish with rice in lieu of more expensive forms of protein. Every home has an airtight stash of this in their cupboard – it's often kept in an old coffee jar or margarine tub.

The more common (and Burmese) name of *ngapi kyaw* simply means 'fried fermented fish paste' – *balachaung*, the name that it's known by abroad, is just a corruption of *belacan*.

Fills a 300ml container

60g tamarind block or 3 tablespoons tamarind paste
75g dried shrimp
6 tablespoons groundnut oil or other neutral-tasting oil
1 tablespoon paprika
½ teaspoon ground turmeric
1 teaspoon mild chilli powder
1 tablespoon shrimp paste (*belacan*)
1 teaspoon sugar
1 x full quantity recipe Crispy Fried Garlic (page 238) or 4 tablespoons shop-bought fried garlic
1 x full quantity recipe Crispy Fried Onions (page 238) or 3 tablespoons shop-bought fried onions

If using the tamarind block, place the tamarind in a bowl and pour over 100ml of boiling water. Allow to soak for 5 minutes and then break up and mash with a fork. Strain into another bowl or jug and discard the pulp. Set the tamarind juice to one side.

Blitz the dried shrimp to floss in a food processor or blender. Set to one side.

Heat the oil in a wok or frying pan over a high heat. Add the paprika, turmeric and chilli powder and allow to sizzle for a few seconds. Now turn the heat down to medium, add the shrimp floss, toss and fry for 1–2 minutes. Add the tamarind, shrimp paste, sugar and stir-fry again for another 5 minutes. The shrimp floss should turn dark brown at this point. Add 100ml of water, toss well to combine and fry for another 20 minutes or until most of the liquid has reduced.

Leave to cool and then add the crispy fried garlic and onions and stir through. Store in a sealed container in the fridge where it will keep for a month.

Crispy Shrimp Relish

PAZUN CHAUK KYAW  ပုစွန်ခြောက်ကြော်

This is a dry condiment, which at first glance looks similar to Malaysian fried *ikan bilis*, but the shrimp floss base makes it much 'meatier' and more substantial, and in fact the peanuts and dried anchovies aren't even necessary. Eat this relish with Burmese 'Biryani' (page 98) or Pork Belly and Bamboo Shoot Stew (page 130) or sprinkle it wherever you might usually scatter crispy fried onions.

Fills a 300ml container

75g dried shrimp

6 tablespoons groundnut oil, or other neutral-tasting oil

½ teaspoon ground turmeric

1 tablespoon chilli flakes

12 dried anchovies (*ikan bilis*) (optional)

1 teaspoon salt

½ teaspoon MSG (see Cook's Note)

3 tablespoons Crispy Fried Garlic (page 238) or shop-bought fried garlic

2 x full quantity recipe Crispy Fried Onions (page 238) or 6 tablespoons shop-bought fried onions

2 tablespoons Fried Red-skin Peanuts (page 240) (optional)

Blitz the dried shrimp to floss in a food processor or blender. Set to one side.

Heat the oil in a wok or frying pan over a high heat. Add the turmeric and chilli flakes to the oil and allow to sizzle for a few seconds. Now turn the heat down to medium, add the dried anchovies, if using, and shrimp floss. Toss and fry for 1–2 minutes. Add the salt and MSG, and toss and fry again for another 5 minutes. The shrimp floss should be golden brown at this point. Leave to cool and then add the crispy fried garlic, onions and peanuts and stir through.

Store in a sealed container in the fridge – it will keep for a month. You can serve this relish as a condiment with curry and rice, or as a quick meal with just with rice.

Cook's Note

Pazun chauk kyaw is one of the many accompaniments to the perfect plate of *danbauk* (Burmese 'Biryani', page 98).

In this recipe, MSG is essential for that full blast of umami.

Bagan Black Bean Paste

PONE YAY GYI　　　　ပုန်းရည်ကြီး

I would say this is the Burmese equivalent of Japanese miso – it's intensely salty and savoury in the same kind of way. I will warn you that it takes a lot of patience and effort. It makes your house stink to high heaven and your reward is quite a modest amount of this black gold, but black gold it is, so if you have the time and inclination (and you live with understanding people), I say go for it. This bean paste, which technically originated from nearby Nyaung U can be eaten as a salad (basically, make the Citrus and Shallot Salad on page 64 but switch this for the pieces of lemon and add a squeeze of lemon juice instead). You can also add a couple of tablespoons to the Classic Pork Curry (page 126) to make *wet thar pone yay gyi* – Bagan-style pork curry.

Makes about 125g

400g dried horse gram beans (*kollu*) or turtle beans
1 teaspoon salt

Add the beans, salt and 2 litres of water to a large saucepan or stockpot and bring to the boil. Turn the heat down to medium and simmer vigorously for 1 hour.

Strain the liquid into a large, non-reactive bowl and then put the beans back in the pan, along with 2 litres of fresh water. Bring back to the boil over a high heat, turn the heat down to medium and simmer vigorously for 1 hour.

Strain the liquid into the same bowl, return the beans to the pan and add another 2 litres of water. Bring to the boil as before, simmer and strain one last time and you'll end up with around 2 litres of dark liquid (you can use the cooked beans in a dal or a salad).

Cover the bowl with clingfilm and leave on a sunny windowsill or in a conservatory to ferment for 3 days.

A white, webbed film will form on top of the liquid (this is what you want – it's called kahm yeast and is safe, unlike mould) and it will also start to smell sweet and funky. Pour the liquid, film and any sludge that's at the bottom of the bowl into a saucepan. Bring to the boil over a high heat and simmer vigorously to reduce to the consistency of runny honey.

Decant into a sterilised glass jar (you'll get about 150ml of liquid) and leave the jar on a sunny windowsill or in a conservatory to ferment for 3 days.

This black gold is now ready to use and will keep in the fridge for 6 months.

Charred Tomato Salsa

PAN HTWAY HPYAW   ပန်တွေဖျော်

This popular condiment is ladled on top of rice and served with soupy curries, such as Bachelor's Chicken Curry (page152). It's made from surprisingly very few ingredients, but it will dance on your tongue like fireworks. It's traditionally made as a smooth salsa, but feel free to keep it chunky. The important thing is to be brave and let the ingredients blacken and burn, as that's the magic that makes the salsa sing.

Serves 4-6
as a side dish

3 medium tomatoes
6 garlic cloves, skin on
3 green finger chillies
5cm piece of ginger, peeled
  and finely chopped
½ teaspoon salt
juice from ¼ lime
coriander leaves, shredded

Place the tomatoes, garlic and chillies on a piece of foil and char their skins using a cook's blowtorch, or under a very hot grill. Open your windows or turn on your extractor fan as it will get very smoky and pungent especially when charring the chilli. You want the skins to blacken quickly without cooking the flesh inside.

Remove and leave to cool, then peel the garlic and place in a food processor or blender. Keep the skins on the tomatoes and chillies, and blitz with the garlic to a rough paste. Alternatively, if you prefer a chunkier-textured salsa you can chop the ingredients by hand.

Scoop out the mixture and place in a small bowl. Add the ginger, salt and lime juice, and mix well. Top with the coriander leaves and serve with bachelor's chicken curry (page 152) and steamed rice, or with any of the fritters on pages 44–59.

Sweet Snacks

A-CHO MONT

အချိုမုန့်

Meals in Burma do not follow the Western system of starter, main, dessert, and if sweetness is required, fresh fruit like lychees, pineapple or mango will suffice. As a result, there aren't that many puddings in the Burmese repertoire, although this is the same for many other South East Asian countries.

However, we do still have a sweet tooth and that is reflected in various sugary snacks, which we burst out with aplomb at festivals, special occasions or whenever else takes our fancy. Outside influences are strong – Malaysian in our coconut puddings, and Indian in our semolina cake and our own beloved take on *falooda* – a wonderful rose-flavoured Indian dessert that the Burmese have wholeheartedly adopted as their own.

Golden Semolina Cake

SANWIN-MAKIN   ဆနွင်းမကင်း

Sanwin-makin is the most popular sweet snack in Burma and like many of our desserts, originally came from elsewhere, as it's based on the Indian pudding known as *sooji halwa*. This particular version topped with white poppy seeds is known as *shwe-gyi sanwin-makin* and is common all over Burma and sold for pennies on the streets. In Mandalay, you would be served *pwè-daing sanwin-makin* (meaning 'banquet-style semolina cake'), which is a richer affair. The Mandalay style of *sanwin-makin* is second only to *lahpet* on a special occasion, and I actually grew up with and prefer it, so if you would like to make it, simply add a handful each of walnuts and raisins at the stirring stage, and omit the poppy seeds.

Serves 6–8

500g semolina
200g sugar
300g salted butter, melted
6 eggs
150g golden syrup
standard (397g) tin
   condensed milk
250g coconut milk
25g white poppy seeds
double cream, to serve (optional)

In a large bowl, combine the semolina and sugar. Add the melted butter and the eggs, then mix well. Now add the golden syrup, condensed milk and coconut milk, then mix again.

Scrape the cake mix into a wok or large saucepan and place over a medium-low heat. Stir the cake mix frequently with a wooden spoon and let it cook for 30 minutes, until it thickens so much that your spoon stands upright, and you can see the cake batter pull away from the sides and the oil rising around.

Meanwhile preheat the oven to 200°C/180°C Fan/Gas Mark 6 and grease an 8-holed friand mould or muffin tin. Alternatively use a large baking dish.

Spoon the mix into the greased tin or dish and scatter the poppy seeds evenly on top. Bake for 10 minutes, and then leave to cool in the oven for at least 2 hours (this will help to set the cake properly). If using a baking dish, slice into diamond-shaped pieces. Serve as is or with double cream.

Coconut Marble Jelly

KYAUK KYAW ကျောက်ကျော

My favourite sweet treat growing up, this is made with agar, a type of seaweed, rather than gelatine, so happens to be vegan. The trick is to get the delicate jelly to settle into two perfect layers and I joke that success depends on the weather, the fat content of the coconut milk and your own state of mind. The name *kyauk kyaw* literally means 'the back of a stone' which I think is meant to refer to the uncut side of a gemstone, but *kyauk* also refers to marble and granite used to make statues, so marble jelly it is!

Serves 4–6

3 tablespoons agar flakes or
   2 teaspoons agar powder
120g caster sugar
pinch of salt
250ml coconut milk

Pour 600ml of cold water into a large saucepan and add the agar, sugar and salt. Whisk briskly to start dissolving the agar.

Bring the mixture to the boil over a high heat, whisking all the time. Once at the boil, reduce the heat to medium. Keep whisking steadily for 5 more minutes so the agar dissolves rather than clumping at the bottom.

Add the coconut milk, and bring the mixture back to the boil. Immediately turn the heat down to medium and allow to simmer vigorously for 4 minutes, continuing to whisk steadily. Be very careful at this stage because the mixture may boil over.

Remove the pan from the heat and pour the mixture into a heatproof glass dish or jelly mould. Allow the jelly to set fully at room temperature so that it separates into two layers: an opaque layer on top and a translucent layer below. If you refrigerate it too early, the separation won't happen.

Once the jelly has set, refrigerate for at least 2 hours before serving.

Cook's Note
Buy a coconut milk with as high a fat content as possible (I find the Thai brands best) as this will result in a thicker layer of opaque jelly on top, making for a prettier dish.

Golden Heart Cooler

SHWE YIN AYE   ရွှေရင်အေး

This cooling snack is served in markets and cafes and even in temples – wherever people need to have a little rest from the heat, there is usually someone serving this golden heart cooler, as it performs much the same function as an ice cream or ice lolly in the Western part of the world. The slice of bread is essential, as discombobulating as it may appear, because it soaks up the coconut milk and becomes wonderfully bread-pudding-like. Sometimes when I'm feeling fancy, I might use sliced brioche instead of plain white bread, but like a fish finger sandwich, often only the pappy stuff will do.

Serves 4

20g dried pandan noodles
   (about 2 nests) (available from
   Asian supermarkets)
½ quantity of Coconut Marble
   Jelly (page 222), cubed
4 slices of white bread or brioche
12 ice cubes

For the sticky rice
75g glutinous rice
120ml coconut milk
2 tablespoons caster sugar
pinch of salt

For the tapioca
50g tapioca pearls
2 tablespoons caster sugar
pinch of salt

For the sweetened coconut milk
400ml tin coconut milk
100g caster sugar

First, make the sticky rice. Soak the rice in a bowl filled with plenty of water for 30 minutes and then drain thoroughly. Place in a saucepan and add the coconut milk, sugar and salt. Bring to the boil and then turn the heat down to low, cover and allow to steam for 20 minutes. The rice should absorb all the milk and be soft and sticky. Leave to cool.

Next, place the tapioca pearls in a saucepan and add sugar, salt and 300ml of water. Heat over a medium-high and boil for 15 minutes or until the tapioca pearls are completely translucent. Leave to cool.

Place the pandan noodles in a saucepan and add 500ml of water. Bring to the boil and then turn down the heat to medium. Allow to boil for 20 minutes or until the noodles are completely translucent. Test a noodle to check that it is soft to the bite rather than chewy. Drain and rinse with cold water and set to one side.

To make the sweetened coconut milk, pour the coconut milk into a large jug, making sure all the cream comes with it, add the sugar and 250ml of water and whisk thoroughly. Refrigerate until ready to use.

To assemble your puddings, divide the sticky rice, tapioca and pandan noodles between four dessert bowls. Place a few cubes of coconut jelly (you can save the rest to eat later) and a slice of bread in each bowl. Now pour over the sweetened coconut milk to fill each bowl almost to the top so that all but one corner of the bread is submerged and the rest of the ingredients float in the milk. Finish by placing three ice cubes in each bowl and serve immediately.

New Year Floating Rice Balls

MONT LONE YAY PAW မုန့်လုံးရေပေါ်

There are three signs that signify that the Burmese New Year festival of *Thingyan* has begun: people start chucking water at each other in the spirit of mischievous fun; the sunshine yellow padauk flowers blossom; and the sweet snacks known as *mont lone yay paw* are dished up to everyone. Similar to Malaysia's *onde onde*, the name literally means 'round snack on the water' as it's made by boiling balls of rice dough, which bob along on top of the bubbling water when they're cooked. The balls are stuffed with palm jaggery, which we call *htanyet*, although you can substitute palm sugar. A few years ago, my family was part of a huge group who made these floating rice balls for the students and monks at a monastery-run school just outside Mandalay. Even the children joined in rolling the balls, and their happy faces as they queued to receive the finished sweets, which they'd helped to make themselves, was a genuine joy to behold.

Makes 25–30 balls

230g glutinous rice flour, plus extra if needed
6 tablespoons rice flour
¼ teaspoon bicarbonate of soda
¼ teaspoon salt
drop of green food colouring (optional)
200g jaggery or palm sugar, divided into 1cm balls or chunks
handful of fresh grated or desiccated coconut
2 banana leaves, cut into 10cm squares (optional)
4 bird's eye chillies (optional – see Cook's Note)

Sift the flours, bicarbonate of soda and salt into a large bowl and mix thoroughly. Slowly drizzle in 250ml of water while stirring with a wooden spoon. A dough should form more or less immediately. Knead the dough in the bowl by hand for 10 minutes (folding it over and over with your hand) until it becomes soft and elastic. If it's still sticky, sprinkle a little glutinous rice flour on the dough and knead again. If you want half the balls to be green, divide the dough into two bowls, add the food colouring to one half, and knead again in the bowl until the colour spreads evenly. Cover the bowl(s) and allow the dough(s) to rest for 30 minutes and then chill until use.

To make the balls, take a small piece of dough, roll it into a ball about 3cm in diameter and then flatten the ball into a disc of about 5cm in diameter. Place a chunk of jaggery in the middle of the disc and then fold the edges into the middle. Roll the dough to smooth it back into a ball so you cover the jaggery up completely. Repeat for the rest of the dough until you have 25–30 balls.

Fill a wok, stockpot or large saucepan with water and bring to the boil. Once ready, drop the balls in one by one. They will sink to the bottom at first, but after about 4 minutes they will then float to the surface of the water to show that they're ready (hence the name).

Remove the balls with a slotted spoon, drain thoroughly and serve on squares of banana leaf or saucers – you're after 4–5 balls per serving. Scatter the balls with the shredded coconut and serve whilst still warm.

Cook's Note
The rice flour adds stability to the dough as glutinous rice flour on its own would cause the rice balls to fall apart in the water.

In keeping with the playful spirit of *Thingyan*, some folk will stuff the occasional ball with bird's eye chillies instead of jaggery and offer them to unsuspecting friends. If you're similarly inclined, feel free to do the same.

Burmese 'Falooda'

HPALUDA   ဖာလူဒါ

My grandmother Daw Tin Tin (my *Pwa Pwa*) was a formidable woman, as were her elder sisters. She ran her own printing press business in Mandalay where *The People's Daily* was produced – the newspaper of my great-aunt, and amazing writer and journalist, Ludu Daw Amar. Another sister of theirs was the cigar tycoon Nagar Daw Oo. Despite her vast intelligence, Pwa Mar, as I called her, was always very gentle and kind to me, partly because she approved of what a bookish child I was. Pwa Oo, on the other hand, intimidated the heck out of me – she would sit there, smoking her whackin' great cheroot, chuckling and making jokes I didn't understand, dripping with jewellery and looking for all the world like a Burmese version of the actress Bette Davis, with the charisma and glamour to boot.

    The first time I met Pwa Oo, she handed me a pair of diamond earrings and then one of her maids brought me a tall glass of this crazy-looking pink concoction and, laughing, Pwa Oo told me to tuck in. The concoction was *falooda* – a wonderful rose-flavoured Indian dessert, which the Burmese have wholeheartedly adopted as their own. Eight-year-old me was completely bowled over. Hopefully you'll love *falooda* as much as I do, although sadly I cannot promise you any diamonds to go with it.

Serves 4-6

1 tablespoon basil (sabja) seeds
½ x 540g tin grass jelly
2 x 100g pots crème caramel
1 x 500ml tub vanilla ice cream
12 ice cubes

For the rose milk
500ml milk
100ml rose syrup

Whisk the milk with the rose syrup in a jug until it turns a violent pink. Refrigerate until required.

Soak the basil seeds in 100ml of water for at least 10 minutes. They should swell to twice their size and become soft and jelly-like and will sit happily in the fridge until needed.

Chop the grass jelly into cubes – the easiest way to do this is to drain the syrup and then use a dinner knife to slice away at the jelly while it's still in the tin.

Now time to assemble your falooda – divide the basil seeds between 4 pint glasses or knickerbocker glory glasses. Now place 2 heaped tablespoons of the grass jelly and half a pot of crème caramel into each glass. Next, add 2–3 ice cubes to each glass and then pour the rose milk on top, filling the glasses by three-quarters. Lastly, place a scoop of ice cream on top and serve immediately.

Cook's Note
You can substitute basil seeds with the relentlessly trendy chia seeds, which unlike basil seeds are freely available.

Coconut Sago Pudding

THAGU-PYIN သာကူပြင်

I have a confession. I'm not the biggest fan of sago or tapioca, having gone through the whole English school dinners experience as a child. So, if you don't make this dessert, I won't hold it against you. Funnily enough though, this traditional sago pudding is undergoing a trendy revival in Burma at the moment, with the most popular brand being a beautifully retro-packaged ready-to-eat number called Ambrosia. And those that do like sago, including my mother, say that this is a very fine version, so what the hell – you might be surprised.

Serves 6-8

For the pudding
150 sago or tapioca pearls
¼ teaspoon salt
200g sugar
1 tablespoon rice flour
4 tablespoons coconut milk

For the set custard topping
2 eggs
50g sugar
3 tablespoons rice flour
350ml coconut milk

To garnish
handful of fresh grated or
   desiccated coconut

Grease a 15 x 20cm rectangular oven dish and set to one side.

If using desiccated coconut, toast for 3 minutes in a dry frying pan over a low heat until golden. Set to one side.

Place the sago pearls, salt and 1 litre of water in a large saucepan over a medium-high heat, then simmer for 15–20 minutes until the pearls become translucent.

Add the sugar and stir. Simmer for another 5 minutes, until thickened. Add the flour and 4 tablespoons of coconut milk, stir again and simmer for another 10 minutes. Pour into the greased dish and leave to cool at room temperature for 15 minutes.

Whisk all the custard ingredients together in a saucepan over a medium-low heat, until thickened to the consistency of whipped cream. Remove from the heat and leave to cool for 10 minutes.

Spoon the custard on top of the sago pudding and smooth into an even layer.

Chill for 2 hours or overnight to allow it to set. When you're ready to serve, put the pudding under a hot grill for a few minutes so the surface browns, scatter the grated coconut evenly all over, and slice the pudding into small squares or wedges to eat.

Sticky Rice Doughnuts with Jaggery Syrup

MONT LET KAUK   မုန့်လက်ကောက်

The name of these doughnuts means 'bracelet cakes' as you make them by bringing the two ends of a long piece of rice dough together, like affixing the clasp on a bracelet. Their texture is sticky and chewy, more like the Japanese dessert *mochi* than traditional doughnuts, and when drenched in jaggery syrup the doughnuts make an exceedingly pleasing dessert.

Makes 16 doughnuts

200g jaggery or palm sugar
groundnut oil or other neutral-
    tasting oil

For the doughnuts
230g glutinous rice flour, plus
    extra if needed
6 tablespoons rice flour
¼ teaspoon bicarbonate of soda
¼ teaspoon salt

Make the doughnut batter. Sift the flours, bicarbonate of soda and salt into a large bowl and mix thoroughly. Slowly drizzle in 250ml of water while stirring with a wooden spoon. A dough should form more or less immediately. Knead the dough in the bowl by hand for 10 minutes (folding it over and over with your hand) until it becomes soft and elastic. If it's still sticky, sprinkle a little glutinous rice flour on the dough and knead again. Cover the bowl and allow it to rest for 30 minutes.

Meanwhile, make the jaggery syrup. Place the jaggery and 250ml of water in a saucepan, bring it to the boil and then simmer for 15 minutes or until the consistency is like runny honey. Set to one side.

Divide the dough into 16 balls. At this point you can coat the balls in oil, cover them with clingfilm and leave them in the fridge for up to 24 hours.

When you're ready to make the doughnuts, heat a 5cm depth of oil in a wok or large saucepan until you can feel waves of heat come off with the palm of your hand.

Take one of the dough balls and roll it into an 8cm length. Now join the two ends to form a bracelet shape. Gently lower the doughnut into the hot oil. You should be able to make three or four at a time, but make sure they do not touch.

Let the doughnuts fry for 2–3 minutes, until they crisp and puff up (but stand well back and be very careful as they will split and spit as they cook and expand).

Use chopsticks or a pair of tongs to flip each doughnut gently and fry for another 2–3 minutes, again standing well back. Remove with a slotted spoon and drain on plenty of kitchen paper. Serve immediately with the jaggery syrup in a bowl at the side, or drizzled all over.

Secret Weapons

There are certain tricks, tips and essential bits that can really make
a Burmese meal. I like to call these my 'secret weapons'.

Chilli Oil

NGA YOKE SEE   ငရုပ်ဆီ

Chilli oil is available in jars from most Asian supermarkets, being that it's a widespread table condiment, but you can make your own as follows. Make sure you have a good extractor fan or have all your windows open, as the initial chilli fumes can be overpowering!

Makes 200ml

50g chilli flakes
1 teaspoon salt
½ teaspoon paprika
200ml groundnut oil or other
   neutral-tasting oil

Mix the chilli flakes, salt and paprika in a bowl. Tip the chilli mixture carefully into a heatproof container with a lid, making sure that there is 3cm clearance above the chilli mixture. Heat the oil in a wok or frying pan over a medium-high heat, until you can feel waves of heat coming from the top with the palm of your hand.

Pour the oil very carefully onto the chilli mixture. The hot oil will initially rise up (which is why you need the clearance) but then it will sink back down and immediately sizzle as the chilli fries. Leave to cool, then cover with the lid. The chilli oil can be kept in a cool, dark place for up to a week.

Chilli Sauce

NGA YOKE CHIN   ငရုပ်ချဉ်

Who doesn't love chilli sauce? Unlike Thai chilli sauce, ours isn't particularly sweet – it's more of a salty, savoury affair thanks to the presence of fish sauce. To keep it vegetarian, you can substitute liquid aminos, or vegetarian fish sauce made from seaweed.

Serves 4-6

3 tablespoons caster sugar
4 tablespoons fish sauce
4 tablespoons light soy sauce
juice of 4 limes
4 finger chillies, sliced into rings
6 garlic cloves, crushed

Mix all the ingredients in a small jug or bowl and set to one side for at least 5 minutes before serving with any of the fritters.

Tamarind Dipping Sauce

MAGYI A-CHIN YAY   မန်ကျည်းအချဉ်ရည်

This tamarind sauce is the default dip that's served with every Burmese fritter. Some people like it very thin, similar to the sauce eaten with the Indian snack *panipuri*, but I prefer it thicker – feel free to dilute it down with water to your preference. You can leave out the fish sauce and add light soy sauce instead.

Makes about 75ml
or enough to serve with a batch of fritters

40g tamarind block or 3
  tablespoons tamarind paste
6 garlic cloves, peeled
  and crushed
2 teaspoons caster sugar
½ teaspoon salt
1 tablespoon fish sauce
2 finger chillies, sliced into rings

If using a tamarind block, place in a bowl and pour over 150ml of boiling water. Allow to soak for 5 minutes and then break up and mash with a fork. Strain into another bowl or jug and discard the pulp.

If using the tamarind paste, whisk with 100ml of water in a small bowl or jug.

Add the rest of the ingredients, mix thoroughly and leave to rest for at least 5 minutes before serving.

Sour, Salty, Hot Sauce

CHIN-NGAN-SAT   ချဉ်ငံစပ်

This is by far my favourite dipping sauce. Whilst it's excellent with fritters, I love to eat it with slices of pork belly that have been poached in a little salt, sugar and water. The Mogok way is to poach the pork belly in Classic Sour Soup (page 88), thus adding extra body, before slicing it and dipping in *chin-ngan-sat*. The sauce also goes really well with roast meats – the pickled ginger here adds a glorious little kick.

Makes about 75ml
or enough to serve with a batch of fritters

20g pickled shredded ginger
4 finger chillies, sliced into rings
6 tablespoons light soy sauce
juice of 1½ limes
handful of coriander leaves,
  shredded

Mix all the ingredients in a small jug or bowl and leave to rest for at least 5 minutes so the flavours mellow before serving.

Crispy Fried Onions

KYET THUN (NI) KYAW

You can buy crispy fried onions in tubs in most supermarkets these days, but these are often coated in flour meaning they're not gluten-free and not as tasty as the home-made kind either. Try your best to slice the onions into even thicknesses, and when you fry them, don't take your eyes off for a second as they can catch and burn very quickly, even at a low temperature. You can toss these on everything, and I usually do!

Makes roughly 20g

2 medium onions, peeled
150ml groundnut oil or other
  neutral-tasting oil

Slice the onions as thinly as possible but make sure the slices are of an even thickness.

Heat the oil in a frying pan over a medium-low heat until you can feel waves of heat come off with the palm of your hand.

Tip in the onion slices and use a chopstick to disperse them throughout the oil. Fry for 5 minutes, just until they start to turn golden.

Drain immediately on plenty of kitchen paper and allow to cool and crisp up. Use immediately, or store in an airtight container for a month.

Crispy Fried Garlic

KYET THUN HPYU KYAW

I've not yet seen these garlic chips even in Asian supermarkets – only crushed fried garlic – so I always make my own. In Burma, they come in lots of different shapes – sliced lengthwise, crosswise (my preference), and even Hasselback-style. They make a surprisingly lovely snack or garnish, as frying them takes away garlic's sharpness and heat. As with making Crispy Fried Onions (page 238), be patient and you will be rewarded with perfect golden morsels.

Makes roughly 30g

150ml groundnut oil or other
  neutral-tasting oil
10 garlic cloves, sliced as
  thinly and evenly as possible
  crosswise

Heat the oil in a frying pan over a medium heat until you can feel waves of heat come off with the palm of your hand. Tip in the garlic slices and use a chopstick to disperse them in the oil. Fry for 3 minutes, just until they start to turn golden at the edges. Make sure to watch them like a hawk at this stage because, if they brown too much, they will taste bitter.

Drain immediately on plenty of kitchen paper and allow to cool and crisp up. Use immediately, or store in an airtight container where they will keep for a month.

'Cooked' Oil

SI CHET   ဆီကျက်

'Cooked oil' may sound odd, but that's literally what *si chet* means. An ingredient used to dress certain noodles, salads and soups, it is simply groundnut oil that has been heated on high until toasty and fragrant. Although often made specifically for the dish in question, Burmese people deep-fry food so often that oil left over from deep-fried dishes is decanted into a lidded pot and kept for this purpose. You can also use the oil left over from making Fried Red-skin Peanuts (page 240), Crispy Fried Onions (page 238) and Crispy Fried Garlic (page 238). A more elaborate version involves adding a pinch of turmeric and a handful of sliced onions to the oil and this is typically used in Mandalay Chicken Noodle Salad (page 117)

Makes 100g

100ml groundnut oil

Heat the oil in a frying pan over a high heat until you can feel waves of heat coming off. Take off the heat and leave to cool slightly. Store in a lidded, preferably metal, container and use to dress salads and noodle dishes.

Crispy Noodles

MONT GYUT KYAW

These noodles are my favourite party trick – the number of times people have actually gasped in awe as they see the noodles unfurl and puff up like prawn crackers. Cristian, the lovely photographer on this book, actually asked me to make another batch just so he could film it!

Use these crispy morsels as a garnish for Burmese Coconut Chicken Noodles (page 109), Mandalay Chicken Noodle Salad (page 117) or any other dish you fancy. You can also simply season them and eat as a snack.

Fills a 300ml container

groundnut oil or other neutral-
   tasting oil, for frying
30g dried flat or round rice
   noodles

Heat a 5cm depth of oil in a small frying pan over a medium-high heat until you can feel waves of heat coming from the pan with the palm of your hand. Break the noodles straight into the hot oil; they will puff up immediately.

As soon as they do, use a slotted spoon to fish them out and tip on to some kitchen paper to drain. Use immediately or store in an airtight container for up to 1 week.

Toasted Gram Flour

PE HMONT

Gram flour is used as a thickener in numerous Burmese dishes, but when toasted, it takes on a fragrant, nutty dimension and becomes a vital component of the classic Burmese salad dressing (see Shredded Chicken and Tomato Salad on page 71).

Makes 50g

50g gram flour

Heat a dry frying pan (i.e. no oil or water) over a medium heat. Sprinkle the flour in an even layer and toast for 3–4 minutes, until fragrant. You must keep moving the pan to ensure the flour shifts around – this will prevent it catching and burning. Store in a sealed container and keep somewhere cool and dry where it will keep for up to 6 months.

Fried Red-skin Peanuts

MYAY PE KYAW

These crunchy peanuts can be used to garnish all sorts of dishes and, with a little salt sprinkled on top, they also make a good snack. I love how beautiful they look, as I scatter them onto various noodles and salads – like perfect little red jewels.

Makes 50g

150ml groundnut oil or other neutral-tasting oil
150g raw red-skin peanuts
½ teaspoon salt

Heat the oil in a frying pan over a high heat until you can feel waves of heat come off with the palm of your hand.

Add the peanuts and let sizzle. Turn down the heat to medium, and fry for 4–5 minutes, until the peanuts turn a deep, glossy red.

Remove the peanuts with a slotted spoon and drain, reserving the oil as 'cooked' oil (see page 239). Leave the peanuts to cool down and crisp up.

Sprinkle with salt and use immediately or store in an airtight container where they will keep for a month.

Shan Fermented Soybeans

PE POTE   ပဲပုပ်

These fermented beans take a little while to make, but are worth it. They impart an earthy, savoury flavour to dishes in the way that Japanese miso does. After crushing the soybeans into a paste, you can use this as is, but in Burma it would be flattened into disc shapes and left to dry in the sun. These sun-dried discs are then fried and eaten with Shan Sour Rice (page 102) or crumbled into Hand-tossed Rainbow Salad (page 76). Before crushing the fermented beans, you can also use them to make a Shan dry relish known as *pe pote si kyaw* – fry a handful of the fermented beans with 3 tablespoons of oil and then mix this with a pinch of salt, some crispy fried onions and crispy fried garlic and then eat with warm rice.

Makes enough to fill a 500ml jar

250g dried soybeans

Soak the soybeans overnight in plenty of water and then drain.

Place the beans in a stockpot with 2 litres of water and bring to the boil. Turn the heat down to medium and simmer vigorously for 3 hours.

Drain the beans and mash gently with a fork or potato masher so that some of the beans break up slightly and then tip on to a muslin cloth. Wrap completely and place in a colander. Leave somewhere warm for 3 days.

The beans should start to smell sweet and slightly fermented and when you unwrap it the beans should have darkened and become a little sticky, resembling Japanese natto, but they should not be mouldy.

Remove the fermented soybeans from the muslin and mash again, this time into a paste. Store in a sterilised airtight jar in the fridge for up to 6 months.

Onion Relish

KYET THUN (NI) CHIN ကြက်သွန်(နီ)ချဉ်

This salad is always eaten with fried noodles in Burma. A 'quick and dirty' version is made by mixing the onion with three tablespoons of tomato ketchup instead of the tomato. It's heavenly.

Serves 4
as a side

1 medium onion, peeled
1 medium ripe tomato
juice of ¼ lime
¼ teaspoon salt

Slice the onion as thinly as possible so the slices are translucent (ideally, use a mandoline). Soak the onion slices in a bowl of cold water for 30 minutes.

Slice the tomato as thinly as possible and then add (juice, seeds and all) to a bowl. Drain the onion and add to the bowl with the lime juice and salt. Mix. Serve as a side to any noodle dish.

Burmese Coleslaw

GAW HPI CHIN ဂေါ်ဖီချဉ်

This is the salad goes well with Shan Noodles (page 114), but is served by default with richer curries and Indian-inspired dishes. It is a must-have for a perfect plate of *danbauk* (Burmese Biryani, page 98). When serving with *danbauk* or other Indian-inspired dishes, you could also add a little chopped mint for extra freshness.

Serves 4–6 as a side

150g white cabbage (about
   8 leaves)
1 medium onion or banana
   shallot, peeled
2 finger chillies, sliced into rings
juice of ½ lime
1 teaspoon fish sauce

Slice the cabbage leaves as thinly as possible and set to one side. Repeat with the onions, slicing them as thinly as possible. Place the cabbage and onion in a large bowl of cold water and leave to soak and crisp up for 10 minutes or until ready to use.

Drain the cabbage and onion thoroughly and place in a salad bowl along with the chillies. Add the lime juice and fish sauce and mix by hand. Allow the flavours to mellow for 15 minutes before serving as a side to any of the meat or chicken curries.

Rice Sauce

KAW-YAY ကော်ရည်

This sauce is a trick we use in certain noodle dishes to provide a silky texture (*kaw-yay* literally means 'glue water') without altering the taste. You can also use it in any dish as a thickener, as you would cornstarch.

Makes 200ml

2 tablespoons rice flour
200ml cold water

Whisk the rice flour and cold water in a small saucepan and then cook over a medium-high heat, continuing to whisk, for 5–6 minutes until it forms a translucent, silky sauce. Keep whisking, turn the heat down to medium-low and simmer for another 15–20 minutes and it's ready to use.

Water Pickle

YAY CHIN ရေချဉ်

This pickle is served by all *meeshay* sellers on the streets of Mandalay. Made up of vegetable scraps (see Cook's Note), it epitomises both 'waste not, want not' and necessity being the mother of invention, which are ardent Burmese practices.

Fills a 500ml jar

2 tablespoons rice flour
stems and leaves from
　1 cauliflower
1 tablespoon salt
1 tablespoon white vinegar
1 teaspoon caster sugar

Whisk the rice flour with enough cold water in a bowl to form a runny paste.

Roughly chop the cauliflower stems and leaves and add to the rice flour paste along with the salt, vinegar and sugar. Mix thoroughly and then pack tightly into a sterilised jar. Leave to ferment in the fridge for 5 days (or in a cool, dark place for 3 days) before eating. The pickle can be kept for up to a week after fermenting.

Cook's Note
You could use the cauliflower florets for Shan Carrot and Cauliflower Pickle on page 197 or Quick Rainbow Pickle on page 198.

Menu Suggestions

All of the below menus would usually be served with plain rice, unless a noodle dish is suggested or another type of rice has been specified. For more, see also page 31 for Eating & Serving Customs.

Vegan menu for friends

Mandalay Bean Fritters (page 53)
Burmese Tofu Fritters (page 44)
Burmese Tofu Salad (page 72)
Charred Tomato Salsa (page 216)

Vegetarian menu for friends

Acacia Leaf Omelette (page 163)
Bottle Gourd Fritters (page 49)
Mandalay Black Gram Fritters (page 54)
Green Bean Salad (page 67)

Pescatarian menu for friends

Fish Noodle Soup (page 107)
Split Pea Crackers (page 50)
Or
Shan Sour Rice (page 102)
Bottle Gourd & Glass Noodle Soup (page 84)
Or
Wood Ear & Glass Noodle Soup (page 113)
Citrus & Shallot Salad (page 64)
Or
Tender Steamed Hilsa (page 169)
Straw Mushroom & Water Spinach
   Stir-fry (page 188)
Bottle Gourd & Glass Noodle Soup (page 84)

Meaty menu for friends

Bachelor's Chicken Curry (page 152)
Crispy Shrimp Relish (page 212)
Charred Tomato Salsa (page 216)
Or
Mandalay Chicken Noodle Salad (page 117)
Mandalay Black Gram Fritters (page 54)
Crispy Noodles (page 239)
Or
Coconut Chicken Noodles (page 109)
Split Pea Crackers (page 50)
Crispy Noodles (page 239)
Or
Shan Noodles (page 114)
Burmese Tofu Fritters (page 44)

Vegetarian family feast

Mandalay Bean Fritters (page 53)
Bottle Gourd Fritters (page 49)
Duck Egg Curry (page 160)
Quick Rainbow Pickle (page 198)
Creamed Corn with Onions (page 191)

Vegan family feast

Mandalay Black Gram Fritters (page 54)
Yangon Chickpea Fritters (page 57)
Green Bean Salad (page 67)
Bean Soup (page 91)
Buttered Lentil Rice (page 94)

Pescatarian family feast

Golden Pumpkin Curry (page 187)
Balachaung (page 211)
Classic Sour Soup (page 88)
Or
Red Prawn Curry (page 173)
Citrus & Shallot Salad (page 64)
Crispy Shrimp Relish (page 212)
Bottle Gourd & Glass Noodle Soup (page 84)
Or
Aubergine Pan-sticker Curry (page 183)
Roselle Leaves with Bamboo Shoots (page 180)
Shrimp & Cabbage Soup (page 87)
Or
Fried Fish Curry (page 166)
Straw Mushroom & Water Spinach Stir-fry (page 188)
Bean Soup (page 91)

Meaty family feast

Burmese Chicken Nuggets (page 156)
Charred Tomato Salsa (page 216)
Pork Belly & Bamboo Shoot Stew (page 130)
Crispy Shrimp Relish (page 212)
Or
Goat & Split Pea Curry (page 138)
Quick Rainbow Pickle (page 198)
Bean Soup (page 91)
Buttered Lentil Rice (page 94)
Or
Braised Beef Curry (page 134)
Straw Mushroom & Water Spinach Stir-fry (page 188)
Pounded Fish Paste Relish (page 207)
Classic Sour Soup (page 88)

Group feasting

All of the below can be easily sized up for big groups and casual dinner parties.

Fish Noodle Soup (page 107) and Split Pea
  Crackers (page 50)
Coconut Chicken Noodles (page 109) and Crispy
  Noodles (page 239)
Mandalay Pork & Round Rice Noodles (page 119)
  and Water Pickle (page 243)
Mogok Pork & Round Rice Noodles (page 123)
  and Shan Mustard Green Pickle (page 194)
Mandalay Chicken Noodle Salad (page 117)
  and Mandalay Black Gram Fritters (page 54)
Hand-tossed Rainbow Salad (page 76) and Bottle Gourd
  & Glass Noodle Soup (page 84)

Simple vegetarian menu

Steamed Eggs (page 159)
Green Bean Salad (page 67)

Simple vegan menu

Straw Mushroom & Water Spinach
Stir-fry (page 188)
Braised Butter Beans (page 184)

Simple pescatarian menu

Po Po's Pilchard & Tomato Curry (page 170)
Pickled Beansprouts (page 201)
Or
Fishcake Salad (page 75)
Shrimp & Cabbage Soup (page 87)

Simple meaty menu

Shredded Chicken & Tomato Salad (page 71)
Bottle Gourd & Glass Noodle Soup (page 84)
Or
Fragrant Cinnamon Chicken (page 155)
Shan Cauliflower & Carrot Pickle (page 197)
Or
Mogok Pork & Round Rice Noodles (page 123)
Shan Mustard Green Pickle (page 194)

Celebratory menu

Burmese 'Biryani' (alongside the chicken stock and
roselle soup mentioned in the recipe) (page 98)
Burmese Coleslaw (page 242)
Crispy Shrimp Relish (page 212)
Pickled Tea Leaf Salad (page 63)
Golden Semolina Cake (page 221)

Finger Food/Parties

'Husband & Wife' Snacks (page 58)
Burmese Tofu Fritters (page 44)
Burmese Chicken Nuggets (page 156)
Coconut Marble Jelly (page 222)
New Year Floating Rice Balls (page 226)

Good to fry in advance and reheat:
Bottle Gourd Fritters (page 49)
Mandalay Bean Fritters (page 53)
Mandalay Black Gram Fritters (page 54)
Yangon Chickpea Fritters (page 57)

Picnics (use a tiffin-carrier, Burmese-style)

Egg & Lettuce Salad (page 68)
Pickled Ginger & Sesame Salad (page 79)
Mandalay Chicken Noodle Salad (page 117)
Hand-tossed Rainbow Salad (page 76)
BFC – Burmese Fried Chicken (page 148)
Golden Semolina Cake (page 221)

Brunch

Golden Sticky Rice (page 97)
Sprouted Yellow Peas with Onions (page 179)
Lime Leaf Pot Roast Beef (page 137)

Guide to
Pronunciation

I'm not even going to pretend that the standard romanisation of the Burmese language makes any kind of sense if you're trying to work out how to say any of it.

Take *kyaw*, one of the most common words in culinary terms, as it means 'fried' or 'fritter'. It looks like you should say '*ka-yaw*' but it's actually more like 'jaw' (as in the part of your body you move to eat the stuff). In a similar vein, there's *gyi* meaning 'big' – it looks like 'ga-yEYE' or 'ga-yEE' but it should be pronounced 'jee'.

This is down to the fact that it's all more of a transliteration – e. g. in the Burmese alphabet, there are characters which by themselves are pronounced 'K' and 'Y', but when you add them together they form a magical ligature pronounced 'J'.

Obviously, there's no way in hell that anyone who wasn't familiar with the Burmese language would know this. It meant that a poor friend of my parents named Dr Kywe (pronounced 'jwair') was called 'Dr Kway' by almost everyone when he came to the UK, which he found absolutely mortifying because *kway* means 'dog' in Burmese.

However, I realise that a lot of people reading this book (e.g. expats or those of Burmese heritage) will be searching for the recipes under the names that this odd convention has given them. Therefore, I have followed the conventional spellings for all of the dishes, but here is a crib-sheet, which should give you a fighting chance of being able to pronounce the names correctly – and also means you can order them if you go to a Burmese restaurant.

Note that in my pronunciation guide:

!	means there is a ghost of a consonant there. It's how you say the middle 't' in 'hotpot' or the 't' at the end of the Cockney 'innit' or the hyphen in 'uh-oh'. It's basically a glottal stop if you know phonetics.
air	is pronounced to rhyme with 'chair'
ao	is pronounced to rhyme with 'cow'
aon	is pronounced to rhyme with 'frown'
ao!	is pronounced to rhyme with 'shout' if it had a glottal stop at the end
ar	is pronounced to rhyme with 'far'
aw	is pronounced to rhyme with 'door'
ay	is pronounced to rhyme with 'play'
ay!	is pronounced to rhyme with 'fate' if it had a glottal stop at the end
e!	is pronounced to rhyme with 'pet' if it had a glottal stop at the end
ee	is pronounced to rhyme 'free'
ee!	is pronounced to rhyme with 'neat' if it had a glottal stop at the end
gu!	is pronounced how a cockney would say 'gut' i.e. with a glottal stop at the end
hb	is halfway between a 'p' and a 'b'
ht	is halfway between a 't' and a 'd'
i!	is pronounced to rhyme with 'fight' if it had a glottal stop at the end
ng	is pronounced like the middle of 'singer'
nu!	is pronounced how a cockney would say 'nut' ie with a glottal stop at the end
oh	is pronounced to rhyme with 'blow'
ohn	is pronounced to rhyme with 'phone'
oo	is pronounced to rhyme with 'shoe'
oo!	is pronounced to rhyme with 'shoot' if it had a glottal stop at the end
tch	is a sharper version of 'ch', as if kissing your teeth at the same time
tj	is halfway between a 'ch' and a 'j'
uh	is pronounced like the 'a' in 'about' – the vowel is barely vocalised and it's basically a 'schwa' if you know phonetics
uh!	is pronounced to rhyme with 'foot' if it had a glottal stop at the end
un	is pronounced to rhyme with 'fun'
!	is pronounced to rhyme with 'cut' if it had a glottal stop at the end

English recipe title (page number)	Burmese conventional spelling	Pronunciation
Fritters (42)	**A-kyaw-zone**	***Uh Jaw Zohn***
Burmese Tofu Fritters (44)	Tohu Kyaw	*Toh Hoo Jaw*
Bottle Gourd Fritters (49)	Buthi Kyaw	*Boo Thee Jaw*
Split Pea Crackers (50)	Pe Kyaw/Pe Gyan Kyaw	*Hbair Jaw/Hbair Jun Jaw*
Mandalay Bean Fritters (53)	Mandalay Pe Kyaw	*Mun Duh Lay Hbair Jaw*
Mandalay Black Gram Fritters (54)	Mandalay Baya Kyaw	*Mun Duh Lay Buh Yar Jaw*
Yangon Chickpea Fritters (57)	Yangon Baya Kyaw	*Yun Gohn Buh Yar Jaw*
'Husband & Wife' Snacks (58)	Mont Lin Mayar	*Mohn! Lin Muh Yar*
Salads (60)	**A-thoke-sone**	***Uh Thoh! Sohn***
Pickled Tea Leaf Salad (63)	Lahpet Thoke	*Luh Pe! Thoh!*
Citrus & Shallot Salad (64)	Shauk Thi Thoke	*Shao! Thee Thoh!*
Green Bean Salad (67)	Pe Thi Thoke	*Hbair Thee Thoh!*
Egg & Lettuce Salad (68)	Kyet U Salat Ywet Thoke	*Je! Oo! Sala! Ywe! Thoh!*
Shredded Chicken & Tomato Salad (71)	Kyet Thar Thoke	*Je! Thar Thoh!*
Burmese Tofu Salad (72)	Tohu Thoke	*Toh Hoo Thoh!*
Fishcake Salad (75)	Nga Hpe Thoke	*Nguh Pair Thoh!*
Hand-tossed Rainbow Salad (76)	Let Thoke Sone	*Le! Thoh! Sohn*
Pickled Ginger & Sesame Salad (79)	Gin Thoke	*Jin Thoh!*
Soups (82)	**Hin Gyo**	**Hinjo**
Bottle Gourd & Glass Noodle Soup (84)	Buthi Hin Gyo	*Boo Thee Hin Joh*
Shrimp & Cabbage Soup (87)	Balar Hin Gyo	*Buh Lar Hin Joh*
Classic Sour Soup (88)	Chinyay Hin	*Tchin Yay Hin*
Bean Soup (91)	Pe Hin Gyo	*Hbair Hin Joh*
Rice (92)	**Htamin**	***Htuh Min***
Buttered Lentil Rice (94)	Pe Htawbat Htamin	*Hbair Htaw Bu! Htuh Min*
Golden Sticky Rice (97)	See-Htamin	*See Htuh Min*
Burmese 'Biryani' (98)	Danbauk	*Dum Pao!*
Shan Sour Rice (102)	Htamin Chin	*Htuh Min Tjin*
Noodles (104)	**Mont Di, Khao Swè**	***Mohn Tee, Cao Swair***
Fish Noodle Soup (107)	Mohinga	*Maw Hin Gar*
Coconut Chicken Noodles (109)	Ohn-no Khao Swè	*Ohn Noh! Cao Swair*

English recipe title (page number)	Burmese conventional spelling	Pronunciation
Vegetables (176)	**Hin-thi Hin-ywet**	***Hin Thee Hin Ywe!***
Sprouted Yellow Peas with Onions (179)	Pe Pyote	*Hbair Byoh!*
Roselle Leaves with Bamboo Shoots (180)	Chin Baung Kyaw	*Chin Baon Jaw*
Aubergine Pan-sticker Curry (183)	Khayan Thi Oh-gat	*Kuh Yun Thee Oh Gu!*
Braised Butter Beans (184)	Pe Gyi Hnat	*Hbair Jee Nu!*
Golden Pumpkin Curry (187)	Shwe Hpayone-thi Chet	*Shway Puh Yohn Thee Je!*
Straw Mushroom & Water Spinach Stir-fry (188)	Hmo Gazun-Ywet Kyaw	*Hmoh Guh Zuhn Ywe! Jaw*
Creamed Corn with Onions (191)	Pyaung-Hpu Kyaw	*Byaon Boo Jaw*
Pickles & Chutneys (192)	**A-chin, Thanat**	***Uh Tchin, Thuh Nu!***
Shan Mustard Green Pickle (194)	Mon-nyin Chin	*Mohn Nyin Tjin*
Shan Cauliflower & Carrot Pickle (197)	Pan Mon-lar Chin	*Hbun Mohn Lar Tjin*
Quick Rainbow Pickle (198)	Theezohn Thanat	*Thee Zohn Thuh Nu!*
Pickled Beansprouts (201)	Pe Di Chin	*Hbair Dee Tjin*
Condiments, Relishes & Dips (202)	**Hin-yan**	***Hin Yun***
Anchovy Dip (204)	Ngapi Yay-kyo	*Nguh Pee! Yay Jo*
Pounded Fish Paste Relish (207)	Ngapi Htaung	*Nguh Pee! Daon*
Paddy-planter's Relish (208)	Kauk-Sike Ngapi Chet	*Gao! Si! Nguh Pee! Je!*
Balachaung (211)	Ngapi Kyaw/Balachaung Kyaw	*Nguh Pee! Jaw/Ba La Chaon Jaw*
Crispy Shrimp Relish (212)	Pazun Chauk Kyaw	*Buh Zuhn Jao! Jaw*
Bagan Black Bean Paste (215)	Pone Yay Gyi	*Pohn Yay Jee*
Charred Tomato Salsa (216)	Pan Htway Hpyaw	*Pun Htway Byaw*
Sweet Snacks (218)	**A-cho Mont**	***Uh Cho Mohn!***
Golden Semolina Cake (221)	Sanwin-makin	*Suh Nwin Muh Kin*
Coconut Marble Jelly (222)	Kyauk Kyaw	*Jao! Jaw*
Golden Heart Cooler (225)	Shwe Yin Aye	*Shway Yin Ay*
New Year Floating Rice Balls (226)	Mont Lone Yay Paw	*Mohn! Lohn Yay Paw*
Burmese Falooda (229)	Hpaluda	*Puh Loo Duh*
Coconut Sago Pudding (230)	Thagu-Pyin	*Thar Goo Byin*
Sticky Rice Doughnuts with Jaggery Syrup (233)	Mont Let Kauk	*Mohn! Le! Gao!*

English recipe title (page number)	Burmese conventional spelling	Pronunciation
Secret Weapons (234)		
Chilli Oil (236)	Nga Yoke See	*Nguh Yoh! See*
Chilli Sauce (236)	Nga Yoke Chin	*Nguh Yoh! Tchin*
Tamarind Dipping Sauce (237)	Magyi A-chin Yay	*Muh Jee Uh Tchin Yay*
Sour, Salty, Hot Sauce (237)	Chin-Ngan-Sat	*Tchin Ngun Zu!*
Crispy Fried Onions (238)	Kyet Thun (Ni) Kyaw	*Je! Thuhn (Nee) Jaw*
Crispy Fried Garlic (238)	Kyet Thun Hpyu Kyaw	*Je! Thuhn Byoo Jaw*
'Cooked' Oil (239)	Si Chet	*See Je!*
Crispy Noodles (239)	Mont Gyut Kyaw	*Mohn! Juh! Jaw*
Toasted Gram Flour (240)	Pe Hmont	*Hbair Mohn!*
Fried Red-skin Peanuts (240)	Myay Pe Kyaw	*Myay Hbair Jaw*
Shan-fermented Soybeans (241)	Pe Pote	*Hbair Boh!*
Onion Relish (242)	Kyet Thun (Ni) Chin	*Je! Thuhn (Nee) Tjin*
Burmese Coleslaw (242)	Gaw Hpi Chin	*Gaw Bee Tjin*
Rice Sauce (243)	Kaw-Yay	*Gaw Yay*
Water Pickle (243)	Yay Chin	*Yay Tjin*

Glossary

Note that most ingredients can be found in Asian supermarkets and even larger branches of Western supermarkets. Others can be found in supermarkets that cater for the specific cuisine, such as Vietnamese or Japanese stores or online (see Stockists, page 263).

Acacia leaf (climbing wattle, *cha om*)
Odoriferous, thorny herb found in Thai supermarkets and used in omelettes, soups and stir-fries.

Agar (agar-agar)
Type of seaweed used to make vegan jellies and jams.

Anchovy
Small fish salted in brine and packed in oil; *ikan bilis* is the common name (originally Malaysian) for the tiny, dried version used in Crispy Shrimp Relish (page 212).

Arrowroot, ground
A type of starch used as a binder in batters and meatballs.

Bamar
Majority ethnic group in Burma making up two-thirds of the country, also known as Burman.

Bamboo shoot
Available in tins and packets, pickled or in brine. Bamboo tips are used in Pork Belly and Bamboo Shoot Stew (page 130) and can be found in (South) East Asian supermarkets. Bamboo strips are used in Roselle Leaves with Bamboo Shoots (page 180) and can be found anywhere.

Banana blossom
Flower bud of the banana plant; sold as whole fresh buds in Asian and Indian supermarkets, or fresh/frozen and sliced in packets in Vietnamese supermarkets.

Banana leaf
Leaf of the banana plant. Sold fresh and folded up in all Asian supermarkets. Used to steam dishes and wrap food or as a disposable plate.

Banana stem
Tender core of the stem of the banana plant used to add a subtle floral fragrance and flavour to our national dish *mohinga* (page 107). Banana blossom is a good substitute as it's more readily available.

Basil (*sabja*) seeds
The seeds of the sweet basil plant, which, when soaked in water, become gelatinous, and are used in Asian drinks and desserts such as falooda.

Bean thread noodles *see* Noodles.

Belacan *see* Shrimp paste.

Bird's eye chilli
Small, red fiery chilli from South East Asia, known as *kala aw thi* in Burmese.

Bottle gourd (calabash, *dudhi*)
Vine fruit that can be picked young, peeled and eaten in Burmese soups or fritters. If allowed to mature, it can be hollowed out, dried and used as a bottle (hence the name). When fresh, it has pale green, smooth skin and white flesh that turns translucent when cooked. Chayote and winter melon are excellent substitutes. If using in fritters and soups, courgette is acceptable in fritters and cucumber acceptable in soups. Found in all Asian supermarkets.

Burmese tofu
Burmese 'tofu' is of Shan origin and rather than soybeans, it is made from ground chickpeas (or gram flour) and turmeric in a manner similar to polenta. The golden tofu that results is used as a topping for noodles in its molten form (Shan Noodles, page 114), made into a salad in its set form (Burmese Tofu Salad, page 72) or transformed into a fried snack (Burmese Tofu Fritters, page 44).

Cha om *see* Acacia leaf.

Chana dal
The split version of chickpeas, sometimes used to make Split Pea Crackers (page 50) instead of yellow split peas. The roasted version is an ingredient of Pickled Tea Leaf Salad (page 63). Found in Asian supermarkets.

Chayote (chow-chow, christophene, mirliton)
A gourd-like fruit, which looks like a gurning pear. Used in

soups and fritters as a substitute for bottle gourd (*dudhi*). Found in all Asian supermarkets.

Chicharron *see* Pork rinds.

Chilli oil
Unlike Western-style chilli oil, which tends to be oil that has been infused with dried whole chillies, Asian-style chilli oil comprises of dried chilli flakes that are fried and stored in the oil they were fried in. Common table condiment, available in jars in all Asian supermarkets, or see recipe on page 236.

Chinese artichoke (crosne, Japanese artichoke, *chorogi*)
Small, grub-like tuber (in Burmese known as *pe poti* or 'grub bean') used in Shan pickles – very rarely available in the UK, but popular in France.

Cinnamon
Fragrant, sweet spice that comes in dried ground form or as dried 'scrolls'. Chinese cassia bark is a good substitute.

Coconut milk
Used in most Burmese desserts. The higher the fat content, the better – Thai and Malaysian brands are best.

Coriander (cilantro)
A versatile herb since its leaves, seeds, stems and even roots are all used in Asian cooking. The leaves are a default garnish for so many Burmese curries, noodles and salads that it's almost a joke, but the stems are an essential part of various curry bases, pounded together with other ingredients to give a green, earthy note.

Crispy fried garlic
Garlic that has been sliced thinly and fried until crisp and crunchy. Used as a garnish. See my recipe on page 238.

Crispy fried onions (or fried shallots)
Onions or Asian shallots that have been sliced thinly and fried until crisp and crunchy are used as a garnish. Sold in tubs everywhere, though note these are usually coated with flour. See my recipe on page 238.

Curry leaves
Small dark green leaves used to give a gentle curry flavour.

Dried is widely available, but fresh can be found in Asian supermarkets.

Daikon (mooli, white radish)
A long, large white radish. Standard or French radishes are a good substitute. Found in all Asian supermarkets and some larger Western supermarkets.

Daria dal
Roasted version of chana dal available in South Asian supermarkets.

Dashi
Japanese stock usually made from kombu seaweed and bonito flakes. Instant dashi granules are sold in tubs or in individual sachets in Japanese supermarkets. A good substitute for chicken bouillon or MSG.

Djenkol bean
Known as *danyin-thee* in Burmese, these large reddish-brown beans are usually eaten boiled and dipped in a mix of oil and salt or Anchovy Dip (page 204). They are also served chargrilled, and even flattened and turned into an unusual dessert. Sometimes small boiled slices are added to *lahpet* and sold as *danyin-thee lahpet*. Mildly toxic due to the presence of djenkolic acid. Unavailable overseas.

Dried shrimp
Tiny dried prawns sold in packets in (South) East Asian supermarkets, used whole or blended to a floss or powder.

Dried chilli flakes
Whole red chillies that have been dried and then crushed. Sold in small jars everywhere or larger packets in all Asian supermarkets. These are used as is or roasted in a dry pan for a garnish, or for making chilli oil (see page 236).

Dried whole chillies
Dried whole red chillies are sold in packets in all Asian supermarkets. Finger chillies are favoured over any other size or shape. Medium heat.

Dried yellow peas (vatana)
The whole version of yellow split peas. Technically a type of garden pea and available from South Asian supermarkets.

Sprouted and cooked with onions and eaten with sticky rice or boiled and used to garnish certain savoury pancakes.

Finger chilli
Long, thin red or green chilli, about the length of an index finger. Fresh green finger chillies are ground up as the base for some of the hot Burmese dishes and used whole in others. Fresh red finger chillies tend to be used for garnishes, dips and salad dressings. *See also* Dried whole chillies.

Fish ball
Asian fish balls are made of pounded fish mixed with tapioca starch and have a springy texture. Sold fresh or frozen (often in packets of 12) and normally pre-boiled in (South) East Asian supermarkets.

Fish sauce
Amber-coloured liquid made from fermented fish and salt, called *ngan byar yay* in Burmese and collected as a by-product from making *ngapi. Nam pla* in Thai, *nước mắm* in Vietnamese. Used as a table condiment and cooking ingredient. Vietnamese fish sauce is most similar in flavour to Burmese fish sauce, imparting the same level of sweet flavour over pure salt. Viet Huong (Three Crabs) is by far the best brand, and Phú Quốc a close second.

Fishcake
Asian fishcake is made from pounded fish mixed with tapioca starch and has a spongy texture. Usually sold in a small 'loaf' or 'brick' that is sliced as needed. Normally sold pre-boiled or pre-fried in (South) East Asian supermarkets.

Fried broad (fava) beans
Broad beans that have been fried or deep-roasted until crunchy. Known as *habas fritas* in Spain where they are very popular. They are widely available in Spanish delicatessens but also larger supermarkets.

Garlic chive (Chinese chive, Chinese leek)
A green herb with long flat stalks, the garlicky version of regular chives. The chive roots (sometimes called leek roots) are known as *juu myit* in Burmese and are used in Shan Sour Rice (page 102) and Shan Mustard Green Pickle (page 194). *See also* Leek bulb.

Glutinous rice (sticky rice)
A type of rice with short, opaque grains, which is especially sticky when cooked. Note that 'glutinous' here means glue-like or sticky, and is not used in the sense of containing gluten (which it does not). Widely eaten in South East Asia, and a staple in Thailand and Laos. There are black and white versions – both are popular in Burma – and they are used for sweet and savoury dishes.

Glutinous rice flour
Ground from glutinous rice. Used to make doughs and batters.

Gram flour (chickpea flour, besan) Used as a thickener or flavouring agent in soups and an essential ingredient in certain salads and to make Burmese tofu (see Burmese Tofu Fritters on page 44 and Burmese Tofu Salad on page 72).

Grass jelly
Also known as leaf jelly, made using a member of the mint family and has a mild, slightly herbal taste. Used in Asian drinks and desserts such as falooda.

Groundnut oil (peanut oil) Used for shallow and deep-frying and also in salad and noodle dressings. Any neutral-tasting oil such as rapeseed oil or sunflower oil is an acceptable substitute for this.

Horse gram bean (kollu) Cultivated widely in Burma, India and Sri Lanka, the beans are boiled and fermented to produce *pone yay gyi* (page 215), resulting in something similar to Japanese miso. Dried horsegram can occasionally be found in South Asian supermarkets. Turtle beans make a good substitute.

Htanyet *see* Jaggery.

Ikan bilis *see* Anchovy.

Intha
Ethnic group based in Inle in the Shan State, Burma.

Jaggery
A solid type of sugar usually made with cane sugar, but in Burma, jaggery is made from toddy palm syrup, which is boiled

until golden brown and then formed into bite-size chunks. Known as *htanyet*, it is considered an after-dinner sweet, but is also used to add colour and to enrich food when cooking. Indian jaggery or palm sugar is an acceptable substitute.

Japanese fermented soybeans (*natto*)
Salty and savoury with an unusual sticky texture. Sold frozen (thaw to use). Traditionally eaten at breakfast on rice rather than used an ingredient, but a good substitute for Shan Fermented Soybeans (page 241).

Japanese pickled ginger (*beni shoga, kizami shoga*)
Ginger that has been peeled, julienned and pickled in *umezu*, a by-product of the production of umeboshi, which are salted, pickled Japanese apricots.

Kaffir lime
Small fragrant lime whose intensely citrussy leaves are used fresh or dried. Popular in Thai cookery.

Kapi *see* Shrimp paste.

Khao swè
Generic Burmese word for noodles meaning 'fold pull' i.e. describing the method for making noodles.

Lablab bean (hyacinth bean)
Large bean similar to a butter bean, which is usually dried and then stored for later use. Called *pe gyi* ('big bean') in Burmese, the beans are soaked and then fried to make *pe gyi hnat* (page 184) or split and fried whilst still dry to make a garnish for Pickled Tea Salad (page 63). For the latter, shop-bought fried broad (fava) beans make a good substitute.

Lahpet
Fermented or pickled tea unique to Burma – we are one of the few countries that eat tea as well as drink it. A national delicacy, which also has huge cultural significance in Burma (*see also* The Food of Burma and Eating & Serving Customs, pages 31–33). The finest young tea leaves are briefly steamed before being packed into bamboo silos, pressed down by heavy weights and left to ferment, giving them a sour and astringent flavour.

Technically called *lahpet so* ('wet tea'), as *lahpet chauk* ('dry tea') refers to dried tea leaves used to make our green tea known as *yay-nway gyan* and *lahpet yay-kyo* ('brewed tea') refers to sweet tea made with milk and sugar. Lahpet by itself though is generally synonymous with pickled tea. The Western world is probably most familiar with *lahpet* in the form of a popular salad served as a snack. Artichoke hearts are a passable substitute.

Leek bulb
Chinese leek bulbs (i.e. garlic chive bulbs) available pickled in tins or jars in (South) East Asian supermarkets.

Lemongrass
Aromatic grass sold fresh in stalks, dried in jars, as a paste or as an extract – the brand Spice Drops is particularly good. Dried lemongrass and lemongrass paste pale in comparison, so try to buy fresh or extract where available.

Lily flowers (golden needles)
Dried lily buds that are sold in packets. To use, soak them in water to rehydrate, then tie in knots and add to soups.

Mango
The king of all Burmese fruits – we Burmese even have a proverb about it. When ripe, it is our favourite sweet snack and when green, we love to dip it in *ngapi* dishes or in a mixture of salt, liquorice and chilli powder.

Miso
Japanese fermented soybean paste used in cooking; the darker the miso, the stronger and sweeter it is. Red miso is a good vegetarian substitute for shrimp paste (see below). It is also a decent substitute for *pe pote*.

MSG (monosodium glutamate – also the main component in Aromat, Maggi seasoning, Accent, Knorr chicken powder, Knorr pork granules, VetSin, Zest, Začin C)
A granulated seasoning that makes dishes more savoury in the same way that sugar makes dishes sweeter or salt makes dishes saltier. Could substitute it with Japanese dashi, chicken stock or Marigold bouillon (*see also* Why MSG is A-Okay, page 37).

Mustard greens (mustard leaves)
There are various types of mustard green, but the one used for making Shan pickles (page 194–197) and Pork with Pickled

Mustard Greena (page 133) is known as *mon-nyin* in Burmese, *zha cai* in Chinese and *takana* in Japanese. Pickled or preserved mustard greens are found salty and dried or sweet and wet in packets in (South) East Asian supermarkets. The Burmese prefer the wet version.

Mustard seeds
Small, peppery dried seeds used to make Indian-influenced pickles and curries. Can be used instead of Shan sesame (perilla seeds) in Shan-style pickles.

Nam pla see Fish sauce.

Nan-byar-gyi khao swè
Burmese broad, flat wheat noodles. Unavailable overseas, but tagliatelle is a good substitute.

Natto see Japanese fermented soybeans.

Neem
A type of tree with bitter leaves. Neem shoots and flower buds are boiled in tamarind juice and water and eaten as a side dish. Pickled neem leaves are eaten with *ngapi* dishes. Sometimes available in jars in Asian supermarkets.

Ngan byar-yay see Fish sauce.

Ngapi see Shrimp paste.

Noodles
Made from various ingredients in different shapes as follows:
- **Thin, flat rice noodles (rice sticks, thin ribbon noodles)** Used for Shan Noodles (page 114) and sometimes *mohinga*; known as *hsan khao swè a-thay* in Burmese, *bánh phở* in Vietnam and *sen lek* in Thailand. Found dried in large shrink-wrapped bundles in (South) East Asian supermarkets.
- **Rice vermicelli** Thin, white noodles; known by their Chinese names of *mǐfěn* and *bee hoon, sen mee* in Thailand and *mohinga pat* in Burma (though technically the Burmese noodles are slightly different as they are fermented – like *kanom jeen* noodles in Thailand). Found fresh and dried in large shrink-wrapped bundles in (South) East Asian supermarkets and larger Western supermarkets. Used in Fish Noodle Soup (page 107).

- **Round rice noodles** (thick rice noodles) Basically rice spaghetti. Called *bún bò Huế* noodles in Vietnam, *mǐxiàn* in China, *meeshay pat* in Burma and laksa noodle in Malaysia; also labelled confusingly as Chinese Guilin rice vermicelli. Found dried in large shrink-wrapped bundles in (South) East Asian supermarkets. Used in Mandalay Pork and Round Rice Noodles (page 119) and Mogok Pork and Round Rice Noodles (page 123).
- **Glass noodle (cellophane noodle, crystal noodle, glass vermicelli)** Thin, translucent noodles used in various soups and stir-fries. Known as *kyar zan pat* in Burmese; generally made from mung bean flour where they are known as mung bean thread noodles, bean thread noodles or mung bean vermicelli. Glass noodles can be found dried in small and large shrink-wrapped bundles in (South) East Asian supermarkets. Sweet potato or *shirataki* ('zero') noodles can be used instead.
- **Thick wheat noodles (*lo mein*)** Known as *gyon khao swè* in Burma. Found dried, fresh or frozen in packets in (South) East Asian supermarkets, and dried and fresh in Western supermarkets. These can be replaced with dried or fresh egg noodles. Used to make Coconut Chicken Noodles (page 109) and fried noodles.
- **Somen noodles** Very thin Japanese wheat noodle usually served cold. Found dried in Japanese supermarkets. Can be used in Fish Noodle Soup (page 107).
- **Udon noodles** Very thick, white Japanese noodle with a square cross-section that can be served hot or cold. Found fresh, dried or frozen in packets in Japanese supermarkets, and fresh or dried in packets in larger Western supermarkets.

Pak choi
Green leafy vegetable, which is similar to chard. Used to make Shan pickles (page 194–197).

Palm sugar
Dark brown sugar sold in tubs, or in blocks that need to be shaved before use. Good substitute for Burmese jaggery.

Papaya
Large avocado-shaped fruit. Eaten ripe as a sweet snack. Whilst still green, it is shredded and made into salads.

Peanuts

Red-skin peanuts are preferred in Burma – these are fried with their skins on and used to garnish several noodle and salad dishes. See my recipe on page 240.

Pickled tea *see* Lahpet.

Pe pote *see* Shan fermented soybeans.

Pomelo

Fruit resembling a grapefruit but larger and sweeter. Popular in Burma as is, or dipped into a dry mix of salt, liquorice and chilli powder.

Pork rinds (chicharron)

Pork skin that has been fried until crisp and aerated so that it resembles Quavers; *kaep moo* in Thai, *wet khauk kyaw* in Burmese. Popular in Asia and South America.

Preserved mustard greens *see* Mustard greens.

Rice flour

Ground from rice, the flour is used as a thickener to make doughs and batters, and also to make rice noodles.

Roselle (hibiscus, gongura)

A plant with very sour leaves and red stems, available in South Asian and Caribbean supermarkets. Sorrel is a good substitute in soups and stir-fries, and rhubarb stalks in stir-fries.

Sago

Pearls of tropical palm starch that are boiled with water, milk, or coconut milk and sugar to make a pudding. Similar in appearance to tapioca pearls and often used interchangeably.

See-pyan

The most famous Burmese culinary technique, which lends its name to several dishes that employ it and results in a rich sauce. Typically, the process starts with blitzing ingredients such as onion and garlic to a paste, then heating oil in a frying pan and sautéing the paste. Next, meat or another protein is browned in the sautéed paste and then water or stock is added. This is then left to simmer until the sauce becomes rich and reduced and the oil separates and

rises as a ring around the inner edges of the pan. This is *see-pyan*, or 'the oil returns'.

Semolina

A by-product of making durum wheat flour. Used to make Semolina Cake (page 221), which is based on an Indian semolina pudding known as *sajjige*, *sheera* or *sooji halwa*.

Shan

Ethnic group based primarily in the Shan State in Burma, the second largest in the country (though still only making up 7 per cent).

Shan fermented soybeans

Shan food found in Thailand and Burma made of dried, salt-fermented soybeans known as *pe pote* literally 'rotten beans' in Burmese (page 243) and *tua nao* in Shan. Often pressed into discs and left to bake in the sun – these discs can be bought online, see Stockists, page 263.

Shan sesame (perilla seeds)

Known as *Shan hnan* in Burmese, a spice that's used to make Shan Cauliflower and Carrot Pickle (page 197). Black or yellow mustard seeds are a good substitute.

Shan tofu

Rather than soybeans, Shan tofu is made from ground yellow split peas in a manner similar to polenta. The pale-yellow tofu that results is used as a topping for noodles in its molten form (Shan Noodles, page 114), made into a salad in its set form (Burmese Tofu Salad, page 72) and turned into a fried snack (Burmese Tofu Fritters, page 44). It is slightly less robust than Burmese tofu.

Shrimp paste

This pungent ingredient is made from shrimp and sometimes small fish that are ground, mixed with salt and then pressed into a pot and left to ferment. Some versions are sun-dried and sold in rectangular blocks or tubs (such as Malay *belacan*). Others such as Thai *kapi* are wetter but are more widely available in supermarkets. The Burmese use *ngapi* which is similar but made primarily from fish rather than shrimp.

Soy sauce Made from fermented soybeans. Dark soy sauce is used to add colour and sweetness in cooking. Light soy sauce is thinner and best for dressings and dips, or to add a salty, savoury note in cooking. My favourite brand of both light and dark is Pearl River Bridge.

Straw mushroom (paddy straw mushroom)
Picked while immature before their veils rupture, so they resemble lightbulbs. Sold tinned in brine and are added to soups, stews and stir-fries.

Tamarind
Sweet and sour pod-like fruit that is usually sold dried in blocks, in which case it needs to be rehydrated before use. Tamarind paste and tamarind concentrate are also available, the latter is preferable as it's unsweetened.

Tapioca starch (tapioca flour)
Ground from the starch extracted from the cassava plant and used like cornflour as a thickener in certain dishes and to make some noodles.

Tofu knots
Dried bean-curd sheets that have been tied into small knots. These are soaked in water to rehydrate them, and then added to soups and stir-fries.

Tohu
Burmese term for Burmese chickpea/Shan split pea tofu (*see also* Burmese tofu and Shan tofu). In Burma, standard soybean tofu (*beancurd*) is instead referred to as *pe byar* ('bean slab').

Toor dal
Split pigeon peas. Sometimes used to make Split Pea Fritters (page 50).

Tua nao *see* Shan fermented soybeans.

Turmeric
A pungent, bright yellow root available fresh or dried and ground. Mostly used in ground form to add colouring and a gentle fragrance and flavour in cooking.

Urid dal (urad dal, split matpe bean, white lentil)
Split black gram used to make the Mandalay version of the Indian *medu vada* (Mandalay Black Gram Fritters, page 54).

Vatana *see* Dried yellow peas.

Water spinach (water morning glory, *rau muống*, kankong)
Leafy, hollow-stemmed vegetable similar in flavour to watercress but sweeter. Popular in stir-fries.

Winged beans
Large bean with an X-shaped cross-section boiled and eaten with *ngapi* dishes.

Winter melon (ash gourd, wax gourd)
Vine fruit that, when mature, has waxy skin and white flesh that turns translucent when cooked. Good substitute for bottle gourd (*dudhi*).

Wood-ear mushroom (black fungus, tree ear, jelly ear, cloud ear, *kikurage*)
A fungus sold dried in packets. Soak in water to rehydrate before using.

Yellow soybean sauce (salted soybeans, yellow bean sauce, yellow soybean paste)
Fermented yellow (actually light brown) soybeans in a sauce or paste. Yeo's Salted Bean Sauce is my favourite brand.

Yellow split peas
Yellow peas that have been split (*see also* Dried yellow peas/ vatana). Technically a type of garden pea and available everywhere. Used in fritters and soups.

Stockists

I live in the sticks, nowhere near any Asian supermarkets. I do my weekly shop at Morrisons, so I can happily guarantee that almost all the ingredients for these recipes can be bought from your standard supermarket. The online shop Ocado has a huge range as well.

The following shops and online stores are my favourites (many of which have other branches):

Burmese ingredients

Mum's House
20 Taylor Close
Tottenham
London N17 0UB
www.mumhouse.com

Bayin Foods
www.bayin.ie
For Burmese groundnut/peanut oil and sesame oil, *lahpet* and the bean mix that goes with *lahpet*.

Japanese ingredients

(e.g. *natto*, wood-ear mushrooms, pickled ginger)

Rice Wine Shop
82 Brewer Street
London W1F 9UA
www.ricewineshop.com

Japan Centre
35b Panton Street
London SW1Y 4EA
www.japancentre.com

Indian ingredients

(e.g. jaggery, roselle, dried yellow peas, dals)

Sathyam Supermarket
18–24 Lee High Rd
London SE13 5PT

Vietnamese ingredients

(e.g. fish sauce, banana blossom)

Longdan
25 Hackney Road
London E2 7NX
www.longdan.co.uk

Thai ingredients

(e.g. acacia leaf, pork rinds)

Tawana
16–20 Chepstow Road
London W2 5BD
www.tawana.co.uk

General Asian ingredients

See Woo
Furlong House
Horn Lane
Greenwich
London SE10 0RT
www.seewoo.com

New Loon Moon
9A Gerrard St
London W1D 5PN
www.newloonmoon.com

Loong Fung
42–44 Gerrard Street
London W1D 5QG
www.loonfung.com

Wai Yee Hong
Eastgate Oriental City
Eastgate Rd
Bristol BS5 6XX
www.waiyeehong.com

Trade Winds
www.tradewindsorientalshop.co.uk

Specialist ingredients and equipment

Sous Chef
www.souschef.co.uk

Index

Acknowledgements

I'm not going to lie – I never thought this book was going to happen. It's been a pipe dream for years and so when my agent Juliet Pickering rang me up just before Christmas in 2017 and said, 'Absolute want to give you a deal', I honestly thought she was pulling my leg. But it was true, and so here we are with *Mandalay* – my collection of stories, recipes and random musings on Burma which has finally been released into the world.

I wouldn't have dreamt about writing *Mandalay* in the first place if it wasn't for my beloved mother and father, Dr Daw Khin Hnin Wai and Dr U Zaw Min. I wish I was even half the chef that my mother is – at the age of 70, she still whips up a daily spread of delicious Burmese food without breaking a sweat, all at the same time as looking after my small children while I'm at work. It was my pragmatic mother who inspired me to cook Burmese food and taught me how to combine all the different flavours and textures, but it was my poetic father who inspired me to love Burmese food and taught me all the rhymes and aphorisms that went along with it. Their knowledge of Burmese food, history and culture is unsurpassed in my experience, and both my parents were indispensable while I wrote *Mandalay*, helping me with testing dishes, reminding me of old stories, explaining and expanding on origins and assisting me with the Burmese names and spellings. So, thank you for everything, dearest *A Me* and *A Pe*, and happy 50th anniversary x

Thank you to my husband Simon for being my rock, for holding my hand (even drawing up a schedule of staggered deadlines for me to ease my panic), for taking much more than your fair share of childcare whilst I worked on *Mandalay*, for making me laugh, for keeping me sane, for loving me and for always keeping me grounded. I love you more and more each day and I'm so grateful that we found each other. Happy 15th anniversary, my darling S x

Thank you to my Mandalay grandparents Pwa Tin and Po Hla Pe and my Mogok grandparents Pwa Aye and Po Thein Pe. You may no longer be with us, but I think of you every day when I set aside that first spoonful of rice just before we eat.

Of course, huge thanks must go to my brilliant (and long-suffering) agent Juliet Pickering at Blake Friedmann who has always believed in me and in *Mandalay*, and to her lovely colleague Hattie Grünewald who is looking after me whilst Juliet is on maternity leave. Juliet, I will miss you, I am so grateful for all the hard work you've done for me, I hope *Mandalay* lives up to your expectations, and I look forward to catching up with you soon.

Huge thanks also to my amazing publishers Jon Croft, Meg Boas and Emily North at Absolute Press who were kind enough to take a second chance on me after giving me my first break with *Noodle!*. I hope I've done you all proud.

Thank you to my most excellent photoshoot family of art director Marie O'Shepherd, food stylist Rukmini Iyer and photographer Cristian Barnett – our lunches together were so much fun and you made everything look so incredible, even when I assured you that all Burmese food was brown. And extra thanks to Marie for making the whole of *Mandalay* so beautiful.

Thank you to my marvellous editor Kate Wanwimolruk for helping make my text so elegant and clear and for being so patient with my (occasionally irrational) requests, and to my inimitable prop stylist Matt Inwood for his impeccable eye and for being so sweet that, when I was unable to join him at the prop house, he WhatsApped photos of everything to me so I could help him choose anyway. You are both legends and such a pleasure to work with.

I've long been a fan of the late chef, writer and TV presenter Anthony Bourdain. The very first episode of his CNN show *Parts Unknown* was on Burma, and I viewed it with trepidation, which quickly turned to relief and even joy. As Bourdain broke bread with the locals, I felt that finally here was someone who had made an effort to understand what was going on around him, and I wept as I watched. I think Bourdain would have liked *Mandalay*, and I had been hoping to send him a copy, but the next best thing is for me to thank him – so thank you, Tony, and whatever realm you're in now, I hope that it's not boring and that there are ample amounts of pork.

Some random thanks must also be made to the musicians Tortoise, Grizzly Bear, Faith No More, Kyary Pamyu Pamyu, David Bowie and Björk, who provided the glorious if eclectic soundtrack to my scribblings, and sustained me even better than the strongest coffee, as I submitted drafts at 2am whilst the rest of my family slept.

Lastly, thank you for the support, love and good humour which have kept me going these past few years from so many wonderful friends, but especially Gail Doggett, Kavita Favelle, Danny Kingston, Aaron Patience-Davies, Anne Murphy, Tim Anderson, Nicky Bramley, Emily Chung, Miriam McDonald, Nikki Barltrop, Helen Zaltzman, Poppy Collinson, Mei Parsons and Huong Black. I hope you know that you guys all rock.

With lots of love,

MiMi Aye
မီမီ အေး

About the Author

Although born at the English seaside, MiMi Aye has spent her whole life soaking up Burmese food, language and culture through countless trips to see family and friends in Burma, aka Myanmar, as well as back home in the UK. A passionate advocate for Burmese cuisine, she is the founder of meemalee.com, host of the supper club and online community Burmese Food and Beyond and author of *Noodle!* (Absolute Press). Grace Dent described MiMi's 'wonderful blog' as a 'compendium of Burmese food and culture'. Tom Parker-Bowles 'loved' MiMi's first book *Noodle!*, hailing it as 'comprehensive, well written and fascinating'.

Having read Law at Cambridge, MiMi qualified as a solicitor in the City before going into legal and tax publishing. She lives in Kent with her husband, her two children and a worryingly large collection of capsule toys.

Follow MiMi on Twitter and Instagram @meemalee / @BurmeseBeyond and on Facebook at facebook.com/ BurmeseBeyond.

Publisher Jon Croft

Commissioning Editor Meg Boas

Senior Editor Emily North

Art Director and Designer Marie O'Shepherd

Junior Designer Anika Schulze

Photographer Cristian Barnett

Photographer's Assistant Guillemette M

Food Styling MiMi Aye and Rukmini Iyer

Prop Styling Matt Inwood

Home Economy Sarah Geraghty

Copyeditor Kate Wanwimolruk

Proofreader Eve Marleau

Indexing Zoe Ross

BLOOMSBURY ABSOLUTE

Bloomsbury Publishing Plc
50 Bedford Square, London, WC1B 3DP, UK

BLOOMSBURY, BLOOMSBURY ABSOLUTE, the Diana logo and the Absolute
Press logo are trademarks of Bloomsbury Publishing Plc.

First published in Great Britain, 2019

A catalogue record for this book is available from the British Library.

Library of Congress Cataloguing-in-Publication data has been applied for.

HB: 9781472959492
ePub: 9781472959485
ePDF: 9781472959508

2 4 6 8 10 9 7 5 3 1

Printed and bound in China by Toppan Leefung Printing.

Bloomsbury Publishing Plc makes every effort to ensure that the papers
used in the manufacture of our books are natural, recyclable products made
from wood grown in well-managed forests. Our manufacturing processes
conform to the environmental regulations of the country of origin.

To find out more about our authors and books visit www.bloomsbury.com
and sign up for our newsletters.